AF322753

NEVADA POST CARD ALBUM

PHOTOGRAPHIC VIEWS OF NEVADA, 1903-1928

By
ROBERT GREENWOOD

Published By:
Fred Holabird Americana
Reno, Nevada

ACKNOWLEDGEMENTS

The author wishes to thank those individuals and institutions who have so generously helped with the preparation of this book. I wish especially to thank those private collectors of Nevada post cards who provided access to their collections and granted permission for their cards to appear in this book: James Campiglia, Paul M. Elcano, James Gamett, James Jacobitz, Martin Kenney, Roger Lauderdale, Ron Lerch, Richard D. McCutchan, Gil A. Schmidtmann, E. Clark Smith, Douglas E. Southerland, Dave Stafford, and the late Anson Reinhart.

I wish to thank Eric N. Moody of the Nevada Historical Society, Reno, who was most helpful in searching out post cards in the Society's collections, and the Society for granting permission to use cards in this book. I wish also to thank the Northeastern Nevada Museum, Elko, and Shawn Hall for their assistance and permission to use cards, also the Nevada State Museum and Historical Society, Las Vegas, and David Millman for their assistance and permission to use cards. The microfilm department of the University of Nevada Library, Las Vegas, was helpful in providing microfilms of early Nevada newspapers. For assisting with research questions, I wish to express my appreciation to the Churchill County Library, Fallon, Nevada, the Douglas County Library, Minden, Nevada, and to Peter Palmquist, who provided information on some of the photographers whose work appears in this book.

A note of special thanks is due the following persons: to Theron Fox, who first urged me to undertake this project, to Paul Elcano, for his continuing interest and for his many valuable suggestions, to Ron Lerch, for his loan of the two early Polk directories of Nevada, to Newton Baird, for reading the manuscript, making suggestions, and helping with the index, to Fred Holabird, for his perceptive suggestions which helped to improve this book in many ways, and to all those interested persons who provided helpful information and encouragement.

When James L. Butler discovered rich silver float at Tonopah, Nevada in May 1900, no one dreamed how significant that discovery would prove, much less Butler himself. It came at a time when Nevada's economy was languishing. The great days of the Comstock were history. An effort in 1890 costing over $650 thousand to pump water from the lower levels of the Comstock in hopes of reviving production had ended in failure. Completion of the Butters Mill in 1900 at Virginia City was greeted with fanfare. But it was built to work old mine tailings in Six Mile Canyon, not to process new ore bodies, a sure sign the flush times were gone. Things were no better elsewhere in Nevada. The mining towns of Austin, Belmont, Pioche, and Tuscarora were in decline. Total bullion production for Nevada had been falling steadily for years. In 1897 it was only $3.896 million. It fell to $3.466 million in 1898, and further in 1899, to $2.714 million. State revenues were down and falling. Investment capital was scarce. The population of the entire state had dwindled to a mere 40,000 people.

Agriculture and ranching had to some extent replaced mining. In the once great mining town of Eureka, for example, a 1907 directory lists more ranches than mines. Moreover, the days of railroad building seemed over. Trains sped across Nevada between Ogden and Oakland, but Nevada towns were generally whistle-stops, not destinations. There was talk of a railroad to the south and a new railroad town few had heard of—called Las Vegas— but nothing had come of it.

All this was about to change. At first it was thought the Tonopah prospects, while extremely rich, were pockets, and lacking in depth. But as prospectors and leasers fanned out over the area and assays were made it became clear the ore body was extensive. Word reached the world outside and a rush was on. Then in 1902, Harry Stimler and William Marsh, who had been grubstaked by James Butler, prospecting at a place called Gran Pah, 25 miles south of Tonopah, found gold float close to the surface. That discovery would prove as great as the one at Tonopah. It would become known throughout the world as Goldfield—the last great gold camp.

By 1903, the discoveries at Tonopah and Goldfield had generated a boom psychology. The best ground at Tonopah had been staked, and claims in Goldfield stretched out into the desert. To get rich you had to get in on the ground floor. Timing was everything. Prospectors moved out from Tonopah and Goldfield in search of new strikes elsewhere.

The town of Ely, the third great mining center to boom, had been dormant for years, even after it was made county seat of White Pine County in 1887. In 1902, prospectors and investors moved in, lured by rumors of vast mineral deposits. Mining companies were organized. Exploration work would subsequently reveal an enormous body of copper ore, one of the largest in the western hemisphere.

These three mining towns—Tonopah, Goldfield, and Ely—would spark the twentieth-century mining boom in Nevada, a period that began in 1900 and ended in 1928. The wealth generated by these three discoveries (which would reach $356.6 million by 1920) caused directly or indirectly the mineral exploration of the whole of Nevada. The result was discovery after discovery, with people rushing from one boomtown to another. In 1903, the strike at Bullfrog created a whole new mining district: the towns of Bullfrog, Beatty, Rhyolite, and Pioneer sprang up almost overnight on the desert landscape. In 1905, it was Manhattan's turn. And the following year there was Fairview, Wonder, Round Mountain, Blair, and Seven Troughs. Over the next five years there were rushes into Rawhide, Gold Circle, Mason, Lucky Boy, Chafey, National, Jarbidge, Golconda, Rochester, and others. In later years the rushes continued, though diminished in size and importance, camps that looked more like automobile parking lots in the desert—Gilbert, Weepah, and the last one, Wahmonie, in 1928.

Bullion production in 1910 had risen to $25.489 million, and the population of Nevada had doubled. During this time new counties and county boundaries were created, and new county seats of government, caused by population shifts created by the mining boom. A dozen new railroads were built, five of them in southern Nevada, and with them shop facilities for engines and rolling stock, division points, and housing for employees. At one point the boom even spilled across the state line into southeastern California during the Greenwater copper excitement.

At the same time Jim Butler made his discovery at Tonopah there was another discovery (or invention) of perhaps lesser importance made elsewhere. It was a process for making a photographic post card involving the use of photographic paper, on which pictures could easily be printed from film negatives. This type of post card has come to be known as the real photo post card, meaning that it is an actual photograph, not a printed or lith-ographed image.

Post cards first appeared in Austria in 1869, in England and France in 1870. These early European cards carried no images, only space on one side for an address, the reverse side for a message. But they enjoyed an advantage over first-class letter mail: they could be mailed at a reduced rate of postage. The first picture post cards appeared in Germany in 1870, and offered images of the Franco-Prussian War. The first picture post cards appeared in the United States in 1873, in conjunction with the Industrial Exposition at Chicago. It was not long before a wide variety of printed post cards were available: advertising, political, expositions, greetings, and more. The post card phenomenon spread rapidly across the world as one nation after another authorized their use. Accep-tance by the public was immediate and enthusiastic. On one day at Coney Island, New York, over one million cards were mailed. Post cards afforded an easy means of com-munication. They were an early version of today's fax message, though slower, of course, relying as they did on mail service.

Most of the cards in this book (approximately 90% are of the real photo type) are real photo, the type with which we are largely concerned. It was in 1902 that Eastman Kodak marketed its post card size photographic papers. They quickly followed with a folding camera (model No. 3A) which was specially designed for making real photo post cards. To make matters even simpler, an amateur photographer could mail the camera with exposed film to Eastman Kodak. They would develop and print the post cards and return them to the sender with a reloaded camera. Eastman Kodak offered two different photographic papers; both could be developed and printed in a dark room using controlled lighting. These innovations in photography as applied to the post card captured the public imagination. It had become possible for anyone who owned a camera to make his own personalized photo post card.

A real photo post card—like any photograph—can be enlarged to bring out the smallest details. On the other hand, enlargement of a printed card will only magnify the pattern of dots in a halftone, or the particular printing process used in its manufacture. The real photo post card has a glossy finish, characteristic of any photograph. For quality and authenticity of image, the real photo post card is in a class by itself.

The wide distribution of post card size photographic stock made it possible for local photographers to make their own post cards. Living in the town, or being on the spot, as it were, the local photographer could take advantage of any number of events: a Fourth of July parade, a railroad day celebration, a fire, baseball game, a visit by a celebrity—whatever might make an interesting subject for a card. Many of the cards have a sense of immediacy, capturing a moment in time, such as the appearance in Ely in 1908 of one of the racing cars in the New York to Paris automobile race, or of Elinor Glyn's appearance in 1905 on the streets of Goldfield, or a large crown watching a fire on Commercial Street in Reno in 1909. As these cards were of local interest and appealed to local interest, they had a limited market. Unlike the mass-produced printed cards which catered to broad tastes and a broader market, they were produced in small quantities. A photographer who made a card of a local event might expect to sell only a few dozen, depending upon the size of the community. A card of more limited appeal—say, of the hometown baseball team—might be made in only a dozen copies. A card made by an amateur photographer showing a picture of his mine or cabin might be the only one, and unique. The rarity of such cards is therefore obvious. They were made in small quantities to begin with, many have been lost because of the ephemeral nature of the post card and through the attrition of time, and they have not survived in great numbers.

The rise of the real photo post card and Nevada's twentieth-century mining boom occurred in virtually the same time frame. The result was, and is, a happy coincidence. Why? Because it gives us a unique photographic record of Nevada during the period 1902-1928 not seen before. Only about two dozen of the images in this book have been published before, and where they have been published they have rarely been identified as post card images. Otherwise the majority of the photographs in this book have been seen only by a few private collectors, who, it should be mentioned, were among the first to recognize their importance. Until recently, photo post cards have not been appreciated for their historical significance. Libraries and historical societies now recognize that they are an important part of the visual record, and have begun to develop collections or add to existing collections.

Choice of subject was often whatever caught the photographer's eye. But there was general consistency as well as variety. Street scenes and town views were popular. Cards featuring Indians caught the public fancy, whether the subject was a Paiute war dance at Schurz, or a group of Indians playing a gambling game at Ely. Storefront cards were another favorite, which usually featured a group standing in front of some establishment, such as the Washoe Saloon in Reno, or a butcher shop at Battle Mountain. Cards showing natural disasters were grim reminders of the event itself, whether it was a flood in the town of Empire in 1907, or the destruction of Mazuma by a flash flood. Advertising cards were intended for publicity; for example, a card advertising transportation to Rawhide from Schurz by Miller & Company. Railroad stations and depots were an old standard, well represented in any post card rack. Boxing matches were popular in early Nevada; there are cards for contests in McDermitt, Tonopah, Goldfield, and the Johnson-Jeffries fight in Reno. Other sporting events were captured by the camera: a baseball game between Goldfield and Tonopah, and a tennis match at Searchlight. Celebrities were caught on the post card image: Theodore Roosevelt when he campaigned in Reno in 1912 for the Bull Moose Party. And in that broad category we call social history there are a number of interesting cards: a group of apple vendors at Bovard, a family dressed in their Sunday best for a group portrait at Prospect, picnickers in a shady grove at Birch.

Where were these cards mailed, and to whom? To relatives and friends all over the United States, and a few foreign countries. While a number of cards were mailed to points within Nevada, the use of cards was by no means an insular thing. And what did these people in Nevada write about? Everything common to the human condition, it would seem. Here are a few examples. A card from a lady in Fallon postmarked September 25, 1907 says: "I spent Sat. and Sun. here with my new husband. It was love at first sight. But I am happy and nothing else is necessary. I know it was rather sudden." A card dated September 14, 1908, mailed from Rawhide says: "This [photo of Rawhide] gives an idea of the size of this place. I'll send a better one next time. Can't use my Kodak here—too dusty, and I can't always get film. The stock exchange and banks here are open until midnight. Hope to see you again next June." A lady in Tonopah wrote to her cousin in Creston, Iowa on October 17, 1907, on a card showing the State Bank and Trust Building: "Would you expect to see a building like this in Tonopah? It cost $140,000 and two years rentals will pay for its construction. All first floor rooms are wainscoted in marble, tile floors, electric elevator, steam heated, and in fact a thoroughly up-to-date building. Tonopah is something else." And a prospector on his way to Jamestown wrote on a card picturing himself, his partner, burros, and prospecting outfit: "On my way to the new rich strike at Jamestown, Nev. Apr. 13, 1908. Frank P. Marisch. 39 miles from Goldfield."

Arrangement of this book is alphabetical by town, from Acoma to Yerington. This allows for grouping all cards for a given town under a single heading. This makes it easier to find cards for a town over an arrangement by subject, which would scatter them throughout the text. It is also preferable to an arrangement by counties, which presumes a knowledge of Nevada counties and towns many readers might not have. At the outset the object was to represent as many towns as possible in this book. For the larger towns this was no problem; there are plenty of cards to choose from. But for the very small towns and mining camps—sometimes short-lived—it required much searching before a card was found, if indeed, one was found. Fortunately, a card or cards were found for a number of obscure places such as Acoma, Aura, Bovard, Beowawe, Buckhorn, Chafey, Derby, Ellendale, Fay, Gilbert, Granite, Hornsilver, Lane City, Nordyke, Olinghouse, Prospect, Ramsey, Riepetown, Strawberry, Transval, Wahmonie, and others. Because cards are rare for these places they are represented by fewer cards, sometimes only one, which means no more were located. The larger towns—Carson City, Ely, Goldfield, Las Vegas, Manhattan, Rawhide, Reno, Rhyolite, and Tonopah—are represented by four or more cards, which is their due, and provides a proper proportion. Towns of intermediate size and importance—Aurora, Elko, Fallon, Wells, Wonder, etc.—are represented by three or four cards.

The earliest real photo cards in this book are dated or postmarked 1903, which is very likely when they first made their appearance in Nevada. But this does not rule out the possibility some may exist for 1902, which have not come to my attention. The cutoff date for this book is 1928, a date that may seem arbitrary to some readers. But it was chosen for several reasons. First, it marked the last boom camp of any size—Wahmonie—and the end of an era before the coming of the Great Depression. It also marked the decline in popularity of the real photo card, though they continued to be made, of course, as they are even today. The linen card, cheaper to produce, had gained in popularity and cornered a large share of the market. The subject of linen and chrome cards and the period they embrace are the subject for another book. They belong to another period, too late for our purposes. Consequently, there are no cards in this book for communities that came into existence after 1928, such as Boulder City, Henderson, Mercury, etc., towns whose beginnings had nothing to do with the mining excitement of earlier years.

For those towns that had existed before 1903 there was a different set of problems in the selection process. That is, cards might or might not exist. For example, it is unlikely cards were made for towns that had been abandoned before 1902—Bullionville, Taylor, Treasure Hill, Ward, etc.—and indeed, none were found. But for towns that were in decline but not abandoned—Austin, Aurora, Belmont, Eureka, Gold Hill, Silver City, Tuscarora, etc.—cards were found. But not in every case. There should be cards for Cherry Creek, Belleville, Garfield, and Grantsville, but none were found. And finally, there is that category of towns and camps that sprang into existence during the twentieth-century mining boom large enough in population for cards to have been made for, but for which none were found: Buckskin, Carroll, Monarch, Packard, Quartz Mountain, Phonolite, Rosebud, Tobin, and a score of others. Hopefully, cards for these towns may yet come to light.

Now for a few remarks about the quality of images in this book. If a particular photograph seems to lack contrast and sharpness it is because the original card lacked those qualities, and a better one could not be found. A card might be overexposed or underexposed, faded or soiled, chipped or torn. Every effort was made to find the card in the best condition, one that would reproduce best, and considerable time and money was spent to get the best photographic results. In certain cases, if a card did not copy well, another card with a different image was chosen instead. Often this resulted in an improvement in subject matter and clarity. There were a few instances where there was only one card for a town, of poor quality and minimal subject interest. The choice was either to leave out the town and card altogether or use it regardless of its condition. It was decided to use it rather than leave the town without any representation. On another note, some cards have been enlarged to enhance details and widen the scope of the picture. Selection was made based upon the condition of the card, the quality of the photograph's composition, and whether it would benefit from enlargement. If these enlargements look more like conventional photographs, the difference is in size only.

Cards were dated by postmark when available, or a date given in the message. A few cards were dated by the photographer when they were made, and the date etched in the negative. For those cards not postmarked or otherwise dated an approximate date is given [*circa*] by referring to the trademark name on the photographic paper, which appears in the postage stamp box on the reverse of the card. Most real photo post cards will have the trademark name of the photographic paper in this space, such as Velox, Azo, Cyko, Artura, etc. Readers wishing more information on this method of dating cards should refer to *Prairie Fires and Paper Moons*, by Hal Morgan and Andreas Brown, published by David R. Godine,1981, pp.187-190.

Readers may ask why there is no price guide to cards in this book. The answer is because any such guide becomes out-of-date a short time after publication, as market conditions change. Instead, a general discussion with reference to grades of scarcity, towns, and types of cards may prove interesting and less subject to change. There are three grades of scarcity used here: common, scarce, and rare. The first point to be made is that printed cards are generally far more common than real photo cards, simply because they were made in greater numbers. It therefore follows that printed cards for Carson City, Elko, Ely, Goldfield, Lovelock, Reno, Tonopah, and Winnemucca are more common than real photo cards, and because they were the largest towns for the period covered in this book, the most common of all Nevada cards. Likewise, real photo cards for these towns are more common than for the smaller towns. However, there are some exceptions, contingent upon subject matter. Photo cards of the Johnson-Jeffries fight in Reno in 1910 are scarce, and a favorite with collectors. Photo cards of baseball teams, personalities, and disasters are also scarce.

Photo cards of towns of intermediate size—Austin, Battle Mountain, Carlin, Caliente, Fallon, Gardnerville, Gold Hill, Las Vegas, Manhattan, Mason, McGill, Rawhide, Rhyolite, Ruth, Sparks, Verdi, Virginia City, Wells, and Yerington are generally scarce. In the case of Virginia City and Gold Hill this means cards made and dated before 1928; cards made after that date are common. Early photo cards for Las Vegas are an exception: any

Las Vegas card before 1916 is rare. Most of the cards for Rhyolite (and for the surrounding Bullfrog District) were made by A. Eugene Holt, who made both printed and real photo cards, his printed cards being the more common. Nelson Rounsevell of Tonopah made about six different printed cards of Manhattan. These are more common than real photo cards of Manhattan, but both are scarce.

Photo cards for the smallest communities and mining camps (any of those not previously mentioned) are rare. For some places in this category there may be only one card in this book—Amos, Aura, Buckhorn, Copper Basin, Columbia, Chafey, Cuprite, Granite, Hiko, Lorena, Nelson, Olinghouse, Oreana, Ramsey, Riepetown, Ruby Hill, Transval, Wedekind, etc.—and these are especially rare.

Most of the photo cards in this book were made by commercial photographers, and a few words about them is certainly appropriate, for without their work this book would not have been possible. Some left their signatures or initials on their cards, etched in the negative, along with a description of the card, and this will appear in white letters on the finished card. Sometimes the photographer's name was printed on the reverse. But this was not always done, and those who did not sign their work remain anonymous.

C. D. GALLAGHER made many photo cards of Ely and the surrounding copper camps of Ruth, McGill, Star Pointer, and Smelter. His earliest cards are postmarked 1907. **A. EUGENE HOLT** was a prolific photographer of Rhyolite and camps in the Bullfrog District. Like many photographers working in small towns, Holt wore several occupational hats—as insurance agent, real estate broker, and collection agent. He was a dedicated booster of Rhyolite and mailed cards all over the nation. Fortunately, he left us a photograph of himself on a post card, which is included in this book in the Rhyolite section. His personal post card albums, and a collection of his photographs, are in the Nevada Historical Society in Reno. **ATHERTON AND SON** were photographers at Elko and made cards for many central Nevada towns, including Austin, Carlin, Clifton, Deeth, Elko, and Wells. In Goldfield, **ALLEN PHOTO COMPANY**, **P. EDWARD LARSON** and **WELCH AND TUNE** made many cards, mostly views in and around Goldfield. **ALFRED L. SMITH** traveled extensively before he settled in Tonopah in 1901. His career began in Genoa, where he operated a studio in 1869. Attracted by the White Pine excitement that same year he moved to Treasure City and opened a gallery in the rear of Henley's Restaurant and Saloon. His stay there was brief, as he returned to Genoa in the fall of 1869. In later years he moved about frequently, from Virginia City to Carson City, Sacramento to Hollister and Bishop Creek, California. In the 1890's he returned to Nevada, first to Eureka and then to Delamar. In 1901 he moved to Tonopah and remained there until his death in December, 1918. His career in Nevada as a photographer is the longest of any of his contemporaries. **WILLIAM E. CANN** of Reno began his career as an apprentice photographer in Virginia City in 1871. Later, he opened a drug store in Reno, which carried a complete line of photographic supplies. He made many interesting photo cards in and around Reno, including training camp photos of Jack Johnson and Jim Jeffries in 1910. He undoubtedly did his own developing and photo-finishing and sold cards in his drug store. In the Reno section will be found a photograph of the Cann family seated in their automobile parked in front of his drug store. **H. LEE JELLUM** made photo cards in the Seven Troughs District, and for Austin and Jessup. His studio was in Yreka, California, and he is listed in local directories from 1906 until 1916. In 1907 he operated a studio in Lovelock. He was apparently attracted to Seven Troughs by the excitement there in 1907-08, and fortunately for us, made a number of cards for Seven Troughs, Mazuma, and Vernon. He was what might be called an itinerant photographer, traveling from place to place taking pictures, consigning his cards for sale in local stores and saloons. **PERCY DANA**, a photographer whose specialty was taking pictures of boxers and boxing contests, took many photographs of the Johnson-Jeffries fight in Reno on July 4, 1910. Dana made a series of some 120 real photo post cards of the fight. His studio was in San Francisco at 1354 Fillmore Street. He was the official photographer for the *Reno Gazette* during the week of the fight. He has come to be regarded as the photographer *par excellence* of American boxing history. His work includes photos of James Corbett, Jim Jeffries, Jack Johnson, John L. Sullivan, Sam Langford, Tommy Ryan, and a host of others. **LEON OAKES** and his wife, **NELL OAKES**, were photographers in Las Vegas as early as 1921, and made many interesting views of early Las Vegas. Their studio and shop was located on Fremont Street, in what today is known as "Glitter Gulch." Many of their cards bear the signature "Oakes" etched in the negative. Leon Oakes was also principal of the Las Vegas Grammar School, and one of his shots of that school and playground appear in this book. He died in Las Vegas in 1932, but his wife Nell continued to make cards into the early 1940's. **N. (NED) E. JOHNSON** probably made more cards of mining camps and boomtowns during the period 1905-1928 than any of his contemporaries. He is best remembered for his pictorial book, *Souvenir Views of Rawhide, Nevada*, privately published in Los Angeles in 1908. Without question, he produced more photographs and post cards of Rawhide than any other photographer. He also made cards for Divide, Goldfield, Lucky Boy, Aurora, Rochester, Weepah, Wahmonie, and probably other locations. His home and studio were in San Jose, California, but he worked out of Los Angeles much of the time. He also took many photographs in Arizona and California. He seemed drawn to Nevada with the birth of each new boomtown, leaving us a visual record of its ephemeral existence. He was there at the end, at Wahmonie in 1928, five years before his death in 1933 in a Los Angeles hospital.

Given the opportunity of time and place, these men illustrated history with a camera, though they probably did not regard themselves as men with a sense of history. The photographs they took of mining towns like Rawhide, Wonder, Rochester, Rhyolite, and scores more that blossomed overnight in the desert, only to be abandoned when the ore was gone, show these communities at their zenith. If mining seems to be a dominant theme in the photographs in this book it is because the mining boom in the early twentieth-century swept like a groundswell over Nevada. Each new boom town contributed to the excitement. There were, of course, communities where the economic mainstay was not mining. There were ranching and agricultural communities, railroad towns, resorts, and government centers, all represented here. One of the fascinations of the real photo post card is the almost infinite variety of subjects they captured on film. This diversity affords us a glimpse into everyday life in Nevada almost a century ago, because what interested the photographer when he aimed his camera usually reflected the interests of the people.

Robert Greenwood
March, 1998
Las Vegas, Nevada

EXPLANATION OF KEY TO POST CARD CREDITS

At the end of each card description in this book there will appear in brackets a key. This key is to give credit to the owner for his permission to use the card, and to indicate the owner.

[JC]	James Campiglia
[PE]	Paul M. Elcano
[JG]	James Gamett
[RG]	Robert Greenwood
[FH]	Fred Holabird
[JJ]	James Jacobitz
[MK]	Martin Kenney
[ROGL]	Roger Lauderdale
[RONL]	Ron Lerch
[RM]	Richard D. McCutchan
[NHS]	Nevada Historical Society, Reno
[NSMHS]	Nevada State Museum and Historical Society, Las Vegas
[NNM]	Northeastern Nevada Museum, Elko
[GS]	Gil A. Schmidtmann
[CS]	E. Clark Smith
[DOUG]	Douglas E. Southerland
[DAVE]	Dave Stafford

1. ACOMA. Located in Lincoln County, 26 miles E of Caliente. Shown here are the crew at entrance of No. 4 tunnel of a copper prospect owned by the Utah & Eastern Copper Company, *circa* 1906. The camp was on the line of the San Pedro, Los Angeles & Salt Lake Railroad. A post office served the camp from April 29, 1905 to December 16, 1907, when it was discontinued and moved to Caliente. [PE]

2. AMERICAN FLAT. Located in Storey County, 1 mile SW of Gold Hill. Ore was discovered here in June, 1859. The Grosch brothers, two of the earliest prospectors on the Comstock, built a stone cabin near here in 1856. A post office was established March 6, 1866. The town was also known as American City, and later as Comstock. In the early 1920's a large mill was built here (shown in this view) by United Comstock Merger Mines, and a spur line of 1.6 miles connecting it with the Virginia & Truckee. Shown here also are company buildings adjacent to the mill. The operation failed in 1926 because ores could not be worked profitably. [PE]

3. AMOS. Located in Humboldt County, 23 miles N of Winnemucca. Card is postmarked Amos, dated 1908, and message reads: "Picture of freight teams hauling freight between Winnemucca to Denio, Ore. We get most of our provisions in this way." The building at left served as stage station, hotel, and saloon. In 1914 there was a brief flurry of excitement in the Awakening District (also known as the Amos Mining District) when expectations ran high concerning what was thought to be promising gold discoveries. [MK]

4. ARDEN. Located in Clark County, 12 miles SW of Las Vegas. Originally a station on the San Pedro, Los Angeles & Salt Lake Railroad, later the site of the Arden Plaster Company mill, which worked silicon and sand deposits in the area, and which operated from 1909 until 1919. The mill was destroyed by fire in 1912 but quickly rebuilt. The company was owned by W. J. Pierce, Los Angeles, and J. C. Gorin, superintendent. A post office was established here in July, 1907. In 1914 Arden had a population of 200, most of whom worked at the mill. There was stage service to Las Vegas twice daily, fare 50 cents. [RM]

5. AURA. Located in Elko County, 30 miles NE of Tuscarora. Gold was first discovered here in 1869, but no significant production resulted. In 1906 the district revived and the camp of Aura received favorable notice in the press. A post office was established July 5, 1906. By 1907 the camp had outgrown the makeshift headquarters shown here, and had a weekly newspaper, the *Concentrator* , general store, school, and boarding house. But ore deposits were not sufficient to attract investment capital and the district faded as a mining center. [ROGL]

6. AURORA. Located in Mineral County, 28 miles SW of Hawthorne. This photograph shows the town during its last and final revival, *circa* 1911. Discoveries were first made here in 1860. For a time Aurora was thought to be in California and was made the county seat of Mono County, California. After the boundary survey in 1862 it was established that Aurora was in fact in Nevada, and the county seat was moved first to Bodie, then to Bridgeport, California. By 1869 mining had declined and half the population had moved away. There was another revival in the 1870's, but again by 1883 the town was in decline. [RONL]

7. AURORA. Main Street in 1910 after a snow storm, yet warm enough for two men and a boy to have set up a couple of drums on a street corner. Were they possibly salesmen—perhaps selling drums—or were they attracting attention for some kind of sales pitch? Above the heads of the drummers at the end of the street is the old Cain mansion, built of red brick and gingerbread trim in the early 1870's, the home of James Cain and his family, Aurora banker and capitalist. The last revival in Aurora was in 1908, and after 1913 the town went into its final decline, except for sporadic workings of tailings from old mine dumps. The post office was officially closed in 1919. [JG]

8. AURORA. A view of Main Street, *circa* 1914. Population at this time was approximately 150. When this photo was made, the two-story brick building at left was in operation as the Warren Hotel. Earlier, it had been the courthouse for Mono County, California, until the boundary survey between California and Nevada established the fact that Aurora was in Nevada, not California. [FH]

9. AURORA. "Freight Team in Front of Post Office, Aurora, Nev. [N.E.] Johnson, Photo." Twelve mules were required to pull this freight wagon into Aurora, which suggests it may have come up the Lucky Boy Grade from Hawthorne. That grade was eight miles over a steep and narrow pass. Supplies were also brought in from Bodie and Bridgeport, but the grade from Bodie, mostly downhill and steep, was also one that required all the talents of a veteran mule skinner. [ROGL]

10. AUSTIN. County seat of Lander County, 85 miles S of Battle Mountain. In the mid nineteenth-century, Austin was the second most important mining center in Nevada, and a rival to Virginia City. The Reese River Mining District was organized in 1862, and a rush into the area quickly followed. It is estimated some 6,000 people were in the district by 1865, and the town of Austin developed into a commercial and trading center of considerable size. This panorama view was taken *circa* 1909. Population at this time was 600. The tumultuous days of its early beginnings were past, and the town had become a permanent, if somewhat more subdued community. At lower center is the International Hotel, its balcony jutting over the street. [PE]

11. AUSTIN. "Public School, Austin, Nev. Photo by Atherton and Son, Elko, Nev.," *circa* 1910. Two boys in the playground appear engaged in a bit of roughhouse, possibly for the benefit of the camera. [JG]

12. AUSTIN. The Austin-Manhattan Telephone Company was organized in 1908, W. D. Carter, superintendent. The company offered telephone and telegraph service to Manhattan and Round Mountain. The Bank of Austin was located next door. [ROGL]

13. AUSTIN. A view of Main Street after a flash flood, taken from a photograph made in 1893. Note the large boulders in the street and imagine the amount of raging water required to move such large and heavy objects. Many store fronts appear damaged; several roofs have collapsed. At right is the Union Restaurant. Further down the street (at right) is the fire station (with bell in tower), and the International Hotel (its balcony extended over the sidewalk). [RG]

14. BANNOCK. Located in Lander County, 13 miles S of Battle Mountain. Caption on card reads: "Nevada-Omaha M. & M. Co. shaft house Oct. 15, '09. E. Goepfert, Photo. Bannock, Nev." When promising gold veins were discovered in Philadelphia Canyon in 1909, a small rush into the area followed. A townsite developed around an assay office, blacksmith shop, and post office. Although several large gold specimens were taken from shallow veins, prospects never lived up to expectations, and the boom faded in only a few months. Placer mining continued intermittently into the 1930's. Most of the people in this photograph are identified in the following card. [PE]

15. BANNOCK. Standing in front of a prospect trench, from left to right are: Judge Parker,
Reno; Mr. Farrell, private secretary to Mr. Mahler; Mr. Johnson, Omaha; Mr. Scharman, secretary to Senator
Ransom; Mr. Duncan; Mr. Mahler in short sleeves, vice-president, U. P. R. R.; Alex Walker, "discoverer";
Mr. Kilpatrick, U. P. R. R. contractor; Senator Ransom, presidentof Nevada-Omaha Mining & Milling Com-
pany, and Nebraska senator. A note on the card says this photograph was taken on the Walker and Neele
lease. A portion of the camp of Bannock can be seen in the distance. [PE]

16. BATTLE MOUNTAIN. Located in Lander County, 93 miles N of Austin. A portion of the
commercial district on Main Street, as it appeared in 1908. The post office and meat market shared the
same building. Note the man holding a dog, and the butcher wearing his occupational apron. Of particular
interest is the display of post cards in the window to the right of the butcher. A number of older buildings
in Battle Mountain were built of brick from local brick yards, a common method of construction before
1900. [JG]

17. BATTLE MOUNTAIN. The Capitol Hotel was owned and operated by William C. Hancock. In 1908 the town had a population of 350, was headquarters for several mining companies, had livery stables, saloons, a newspaper,*The Battle Mountain Free Press*, assay offices, churches, a soda water plant, a milliner, doctor, school, and railroad shops for the Nevada Central Railroad. The town took its name after a skirmish between overland emigrants and Shoshone Indians in 1857. This card was made by Long & Osborne, photographers, of Evanston, Wyoming, *circa* 1908, as well as the following card. [RG]

18. BATTLE MOUNTAIN. In the early days Battle Mountain was the northern terminus of the Nevada Central Railroad, which ran a distance of 93 miles to Austin, the county seat. Its charter expired in 1938 and the line was discontinued. Another early line, the 12-mile Battle Mountain and Lewis Railroad was completed July, 1881, and ran to the mining town of Lewis. The property of this line was sold when operations were discontinued in March, 1882. Battle Mountain was also a station on the main line of the Western Pacific, also the Southern Pacific. [RG]

19. BATTLE MOUNTAIN. A group of local lounge-lizards gathered in front of the Nevada Hotel, 1910. The hotel was owned and operated by Fred Altenber. Two men at right of doorway under the Schlitz Beer sign are filling glasses with a liquid refreshment. [PE]

20. BEATTY. Located in Nye County, 75 miles SE of Goldfield. The Montgomery Hotel offered the best accommodations in the Bullfrog District, a telephone and bath in every room. It was built in 1905 by Bob Montgomery, who developed the Johnnie Mine, and who staked out the famous Montgomery-Shoshone Mine at Rhyolite. He later sold his interest in the Montgomery-Shoshone to steel tycoon Charles Schwab. The hotel was dismantled and moved to Pioneer in 1908, and was burned to the ground in 1909. [PE]

21. BEATTY. A photograph taken on Main Street in Beatty, *circa* 1908. The men in this picture are posed as though for a studio photograph, dressed in suits, ties, hats, one carrying a cane, one comically mounted on a burro. The wagon and burro may have been part of the photographer's equipment, used for taking outdoor pictures. In the background at left by the lady with a parasol is what appears to be the back portion of a van, on which are displayed photographs and post cards. Inside the van there was probably a dark room for developing and photo finishing. The van suggests an itinerant photographer, one who set up shop on weekends or holidays, then moved on. [PE]

22. BEATTY. "Indians living near Beatty, Nev.," *circa* 1908 by A. E. Holt, of Rhyolite. During the Bullfrog excitement, Paiute and Shoshone women earned a few dollars selling pine nuts and woven baskets, and taking in laundry from the miners. Except for the shoes, the clothing worn by the women here appears to be traditional Paiute, including the blankets. [PE]

23. BEATTY. A photograph of Remick's Garage taken by N. E. Johnson at the time of the Wahmonie excitement in 1928. Note the sign "Wahmonie" above the Union gasoline sign in center. N. E. Johnson had a talent for including crowds of people in his photographs, a technique found in his photos of Rawhide, Weepah, and Wahmonie. Beatty and Indian Springs were the last gasoline stops on the route to Wahmonie. [JG]

24. BELMONT. Located in Nye County, 48 miles N of Tonopah. A rare view of Main Street, done by Osborn & Skinner, photographers, of Tonopah, *circa* 1905. Belmont had been one of the great mining centers of nineteenth-century Nevada. But by 1906 Belmont had seen her glory fade. Most of the large mines had closed, and only a few small operations continued. The general election of 1903 listed only 36 registered voters. The town had a brief revival in 1907-08, when tailings from old mine dumps were worked, and the population rose briefly to 200. At this time there was daily stage service to Manhattan and Tonopah, fare $2.50. [RG]

25. BELMONT. Belmont had its beginnings in 1865, when rich silver ore was found. It was thought a second Comstock Lode had been discovered, and the town boomed. By 1867, some 6,000 people had arrived. Brick and stone buildings went up, an opera house, mills, restaurants, an oyster bar, bakeries, newspapers, churches, schools and fraternal organizations. The mines continued to work around the clock. For a time it was the largest town in eastern Nevada, with a population estimated near 10,000. By 1885 some $15 million in silver and lead had been produced. This bird's-eye view shows Belmont shortly after the turn of the century. [NHS]

26. BELMONT. Originally the county seat of Nye County, the courthouse shown here was built in 1874. The bricks and lime used in its construction were all fired in Belmont kilns, and the stone used in its foundation was hand-quarried in a nearby canyon. There was a stairway from the second floor to the cupola on top, from which one got a splendid view of the town. With the rise of Tonopah, the county seat was moved there in 1904, and the building at Belmont was abandoned. This view shows a group of locals posing at the entrance, *circa* 1906. Note the boarded-up window at lower right. [RG]

27. BEOWAWE. Located in Eureka County, 38 miles E of Battle Mountain. Shown here is the Southern Pacific Railroad depot, with a freighter and 10-horse team at the loading dock. Beowawe had been a station on the old Central Pacific as early as 1868. The Horseshoe Ranch, one of the largest cattle ranches in central Nevada, is located here. The area was originally a Paiute campsite, abundant with deer and antelope. Beowawe is located in one of the most picturesque valleys in Nevada. [RONL]

28. BERLIN. Located in Nye County, 4 miles S of Ione. The mill shown in the foreground was owned by the Nevada Company, a property of John Stokes, eastern capitalist. It was built when the machinery of the old Pioneer and Knickerbocker Mills was moved from Ione to Berlin in 1898, and a new 30-stamp mill erected here. The mill continued to operate intermittently over the next decade, processing ores for mines in the district. A portion of the townsite can be seen in the distance. Date of this card is *circa* 1905. [NHS]

29. BERLIN. In 1954 the moribund town of Berlin made national news when Dr. Charles Camp and a team of paleontologists uncovered the fossil remains of a giant ichthyosaur, a prehistoric sea creature fifty to sixty feet in length, literally a sea dragon. Fragments of other such creatures were uncovered in the surrounding area. As a result of the discovery, Berlin has been a state park since 1955, where tours and exhibits feature a fossil shed, and various aspects of mining life at the turn of the century. [NHS] Date of this card is *circa* 1906.

30. BIRCH. Located in Eureka County, 26 miles NE of Eureka. This settlement was named in honor of James E. Birch, pioneer stagecoach driver in California and Nevada. Photo shows a large group of people gathered in a shady grove. Card is dated March 11, 1911. Written to Kate Moorehead in Eureka, the message reads: "Having heard you say you did not have one of the picnic pictures, and as I have one to spare, thought I would send it. Grace Jacobsen." [JG]

31. BIRCH. Message on card reads: "This is a mine about 5 miles east from where I live. They just start-ed to work last summer but quit for the winter, will start to work early this spring . . . Fred B. Crofut, Birch, Eureka Co., Nevada." View shows men standing around a shaft and hoist, a large bucket suspended in hoist by a wire cable. The bucket was probably used to lower men down into the shaft as well as to bring up ore from below. [PE]

32. BLACK CANYON. Located in Pershing County. This property was owned by A. Borland, who was president of the First National Bank of Lovelock. Photo shows tents on steep hillside, conditions typical for miners and prospectors who journeyed out into the most remote places, often many miles from a doc-tor, dentist, post office, and store. Prospectors often traveled into areas where there were no roads or bridges, carrying their supplies either by autos or burros, often at the mercy of sudden flash floods, bliz-zards, or extremes of temperature. [RG]

33. BLAIR. Located in Esmeralda County, 2 miles N of Silver Peak, 40 miles SW of Goldfield. Blair was nearing the peak of its boom when this photograph was made, *circa* 1909, with a population of 1,000. There were two newspapers, churches, school, water and sewage system, a variety of stores, the Blair Booster Club, bakery, news agency, ice house, electric power company, livery stables, bank, and ten saloons. The Silver Peak Railroad was completed in October, 1906, a 17-mile line that ran from Blair to Blair Junction, where it connected with the Tonopah & Goldfield line. A post office was established in November, 1906, and discontinued December, 1916. [RONL]

34. BLAIR. Card is postmarked Blair and is dated July 19, 1909. The writer has identified seven points of interest, including a view of his house, the Blair Hotel, fire station, Silver Peak Railroad depot, etc., with numbers written on the appropriate buildings as a key. Message reads: "Dear Aunt Lizzie. Can you imagine this place in the fierce, glaring heat of the desert? Even the dwarf sagebrush is burned to a crisp and we look like Indians. Are we downhearted? No." [PE]

35. BLAIR. This mine began operations at Blair in 1907, and for a time it was the largest operating mill in Nevada. It was one of the first mines to install an electric locomotive using the trolley system to remove ore from the mine. In 1908 the mine produced $700,000. The Silver Peak Railroad, when it was completed in 1906, facilitated operations with reduced shipping rates. In its ten years of operation, the mine produced some $7 million. [RG]

36. BLAIR. The Blair Hotel was owned and operated by G. J. Crumbley. By 1911 it was gone, destroyed by fire. By 1916 the Pittsburgh Silver Peak Mine had closed. Population had fallen from 1,000 in 1909 to a mere 100 in 1914, and only two saloons were still open. Two years later the huge mill at the Pittsburgh Mine was dismantled, the track of the Silver Peak Railroad torn out for salvage, and the town abandoned. [RONL]

37. BOVARD. Located in Mineral County, 15 miles SW of Rawhide, 23 miles NE of Hawthorne. This rare card shows the fledgling camp of Bovard, only two days old. Some 800 people rushed to the new camp in the spring and summer of 1908. Many of these hopefuls were from nearby Rawhide, who made the journey by whatever means to the new El Dorado. But Bovard was ephemeral; it didn't last long enough to qualify for a post office. Its sister camp of Lorena, a mile or so down the road, vanished even quicker than Bovard. Note the autos parked on Bovard's "Main Street." [RG]

38. BOVARD. Caption on card reads: "Early Days in Bovard, April 28,1908. Osborn Photo." A group of Bovard adventurers gather around an apple vendor's display for their photograph. The apples were most probably brought into the camp from either Rawhide or Hawthorne. During the summer of 1908, rainbow-chasers thronged into Bovard, and town lots sold briskly, for as much as $100 a front foot. But the people rushed out almost as quickly as they had come. There was no ore to support a camp, not even a tent town. By the end of 1908 the boom was a bust. [NHS]

39. BOVARD. "Early Days in Bovard, April 28,1908. Osborn Photo." Another view, taken on the same day as the preceding card, showing some of the adventurers that had rushed to Bovard seeking their fortune. Note the wooden building at left with "Rooms" painted on side, old automobile at right, and two ladies in picture. [PE]

40. BUCKHORN. Located in Eureka County, 35 miles SSW of Palisade. Gold deposits were discovered here in 1908 by Joseph Lynn, who sold his interests to George Wingfield of Goldfield fame. Wingfield built an electric generating plant to supply power for a 300-ton mill. By 1916 the ore was mined out and the mill was dismantled. In its brief life, Buckhorn was home for some 300 people, had stores, saloons, hotel, restaurant, and regular stage service. Total production of the mines in the district was $1.1 million. The post office was opened February 18, 1910, and discontinued May 15, 1916. Card is postmarked Buckhorn, dated May 15, 1914. [RG]

41. BULLFROG. Located in Nye County, 1 mile SW of Rhyolite. Gold was discovered here in August, 1904, by "Shorty" Harris and Eddie Cross. They named the mine and district Bullfrog for the mottled green rock that resembled the coloring of a bullfrog. In the fall of 1904 over 1,000 people arrived. Within a year the camp had a bank, auto supply store, telephone exchange, laundry, restaurant, saloons, and the law office of William M. Stewart, retired Nevada senator. For a short time Bullfrog and Rhyolite contended for dominance in the district, but by 1906 Rhyolite was clearly the favorite, and when the railroads came to Rhyolite, it emerged the winner. This view of Main Street is *circa* 1906. [NHS]

42. BULLFROG. "Bullfrog, Nevada, November, 1906," photograph by A. E. Holt, of Rhyolite. The tents at lower right are where Bullfrog merged into the south end of Rhyolite. The name Bullfrog was also given to Bullfrog Mountain, site of the Original Bullfrog Mine, where "Shorty" Harris and Eddie Cross made their discovery, and to the Bullfrog Mining District, which included the towns of Beatty, Rhyolite, Bullfrog, Pioneer, and Amargosa City. [NHS]

43. CALIENTE. Located in Lincoln County, 25 miles S of Pioche. Card is dated October, 1910, and shows shops and yards of the San Pedro, Los Angeles & Salt Lake Railroad in foreground, town at left center. The town was first settled in 1901 and named after hot springs in the area. Caliente was an important division point on the railroad, with a roundhouse, switching yards, and company housing for its many employees. The fortunes of the town often rose and fell with those of the railroad. The construction of the railroad across southern Nevada was plagued with washouts and floods. When these occurred, large construction gangs were assembled here and housed temporarily. [RG]

44. CALIENTE. Date of this card is *circa* 1910, and shows a row of commercial buildings fronting the railroad track. Population at this time was 400. When the townsite was originally laid out the place was called Calientes, but it was changed by postal authorities to Caliente when a post office was opened in August, 1901. In 1910 the town had a school, bank, stores, undertaker, newspaper, opera house, hotel, bakery, laundry, ice house and dairy, physician, dentist, druggist, and the usual assortment of saloons. [PE]

45. CALIENTE. A view of Main Street, *circa* 1925, showing the Rex Theater at left (with Marion Davies posters on the sidewalk), post office, Caliente Garage, Caliente Pool Hall, a general merchandise store, and drug store at the end of the block. Note the old style gasoline pumps on the street. [ROGL]

46. CALIENTE. The San Pedro, Los Angeles & Salt Lake Railroad depot after the great flood of 1910. The depot, which had been completed only a short time before, was structurally damaged. The round-house was completely underwater. The flood was so devastating that the eastbound Los Angeles Limited was forced to stop at Las Vegas on December 31,1909. It did not reach Salt Lake City until six months later, because bridges and long sections of track had been swept away by the flood. [PE]

47. CANDELARIA. Located in Mineral County, 23 miles S of Mina, near Columbus. This card was made from a photograph taken in 1893. Silver was discovered here in 1863, but it was not until 1873, when the Northern Belle Mine began operating, that a settlement began. A townsite took shape in 1875, and by 1880 there was a population of 1,500. In 1882 the Carson & Colorado Railroad reached Candelaria. The Northern Belle and the Vanderbilt were the most important mining properties. Total production for the district is estimated at $13.891 million between 1873 and 1940. The large building on the hill at end of street (in center of view) is the Princess Mill. [NHS]

48. CARLIN. Located in Elko County, 24 miles SW of Elko. This card is *circa* 1911, when the population was around 600. The Overland Hotel is shown at right. The community had 3 hotels, restaurants, stores, drug store, two Chinese stores, bakery, school, and eight saloons. A post office was established December 4, 1868. The town was originally settled in the early 1860's by J. A. Palmer, and named by railroad officials for William P. Carlin, an officer in the Union Army. [RONL]

49. CARLIN. The depot shown here was built by the Southern Pacific Railroad in 1906. The top floor contained living quarters for the station master. The ground floor housed a waiting room, ticket and tele-graph office. In the basement there was a kitchen and dining room. The building was razed in 1962. Carlin was the first railroad station east of Sparks where refrigeration cars were re-stocked with ice. There was a pond on the outskirts of town, and ice blocks were cut in winter, sometimes four feet thick, and stored in an ice house for use during summer months.[RONL]

50. CARLIN. The new shop buildings and roundhouse of the Southern Pacific Railroad were built in 1911, making Carlin one of the important division points on the line. This card is by Long & Osborne of Evanston, Wyoming, who made a series of real photo cards of northeastern Nevada towns in 1911. [MK]

51. CARRARA. Located in Nye County 9 miles S of Beatty. Named after a marble-bearing region in northwestern Italy, marble was first quarried here in 1904 by the American Carrara Marble Company. Additional deposits were discovered in 1911, a cable railway built for moving workers and marble slabs to and from the quarry, and a townsite laid out in 1913. Population at that time was 100. The town was a station on the Las Vegas & Tonopah Railroad, had electric power, a hotel and restaurant, newspaper, saloons, and the Carrara Amusement Company. Quarry operations ceased in the early 1920's when the quality of marble deteriorated, and the post office was closed in September, 1924. [NHS]

52. CARSON CITY. State Capitol of Nevada and county seat of Ormsby County. This photo card shows the capitol *circa* 1910, with row of commercial buildings at left. As the center of state government, the town at this time was a stable community, not dependent upon the boom and bust cycles of mining towns. The U. S. Mint branch had begun production in 1870, the State Orphan's Home opened in 1870, and the State Prison in 1867. The Virginia & Truckee Railroad maintained its shops and offices in Carson City. It was also the county seat of Ormsby County until 1969, when the county and Carson City were consolidated into one governmental unit. [RG]

53. CARSON CITY. "B. [sic] and T. Depot, Carson City, Nevada." Card is dated 1913 and shows engine no. 11 at right, built by Baldwin Locomotive Co. in 1872. No. 11 was a workhorse engine for the Virginia & Truckee Railroad, running on the Minden line as late as 1941. The depot is at left of view. The Virginia & Truckee shops, turntable, foundry, forging shops, power house, freight warehouse, and offices were all located in Carson City. [PE]

54. CARSON CITY. View shows the office of the *Carson City News, circa* 1908. The people in the photograph are unidentified. The editor of the newspaper in 1908 was Walter McClure Gottwaldt, and the paper was owned by the Nevada Press Company. The paper commenced publication on June 21, 1891. From 1892 until 1895 it was owned by Anne Martin, leading Nevada suffragette, and a candidate for U. S. Senate. The boy in the picture is possibly the newsboy for the *News* . [JG]

55. CARSON CITY. The U. S. Mint was established in 1866, and in 1870 began minting silver and gold coins, including silver dollars, double and half eagles. Later, silver dimes, twenty cent pieces, quarters, and half dollars were minted. The mint was closed in 1893 when gold and silver production on the Comstock declined. Between 1893 and 1939 the building was used for various purposes. In 1939 it was acquired by the State of Nevada for a museum. It has since attracted a large number of visitors and regularly displays exhibits of historical artifacts. [JG]

56. CARSON CITY. View shows a portion of the Nevada State Prison and yard. The buildings were built with stone from a quarry on the site. While the stone was being cut, a number of fossil imprints were discovered, such as those of a mastodon, and of birds. But the most interesting was a fossil imprint that closely resembled the footprint of a prehistoric man. Anthropologists argued over the imprint for some forty years, whether the print was made by a man or animal. Today it is generally considered to be the imprint made by a prehistoric sloth. [RONL]

57. CHAFEY. Located in Pershing County, 20 miles SW of Winnemucca. Originally called Dun Glen, a mining camp that existed from 1862 until 1894, Chafey was built on the site of the old camp in 1908. The town enjoyed a revival of mining in 1908 and 1,000 people arrived, each hoping to strike a bonanza. During its brief existence Chafey had a newspaper, saloons, hotel, and stores. A post office was established August 4,1908, but closed April 15, 1913. The most productive mine in the camp was the Chafey Mine, owned by E. S. Chafey, for whom the town was named. Work at the mine ceased in 1913 and the town went into rapid decline. By 1914 only two small lease operations were still active. [RG]

58. CLIFTON. Located in Lander County, 1 mile W of Austin. Caption on the card reads "Austin, Nev." but this is actually Clifton. A view of the Nevada Central Railroad buildings and depot. The people at left center are spectators watching a baseball game. At top center is the Austin Silver Mining Company mill and tailing dump. At center are the freight buildings of the Nevada Central, and at bottom, the engine house, turntable and depot. At this time, *circa* 1908, the Nevada Central was owned by Anson Stokes. [ROGL]

59. CLIFTON. Caption on card reads: "Austin, Nev." but this actually is Clifton. Shown here is the mill of the Austin Silver Mining Company built by Anson Stokes, eastern capitalist, who spent much of his personal fortune in a failed effort to revitalize silver mining in the Austin district. Earlier in the 1860's, Clifton had been a mining town in its own right and a rival to nearby Austin, with hotels, restaurants, Wells Fargo Agency, mining recorder, etc. But it quickly lost out to Austin. In 1864 its post office was discontinued. At the turn of the century it revived briefly when it became the southern terminus of the Nevada Central Railroad. [RONL]

60. COALDALE. Located in Esmeralda County, 6.3 miles E of Blair Junction. Card is dated June 22, 1911, and shows an operating coal mine. Deposits of bituminous coal were found here in the 1890's by William Groezinger. In 1903 a townsite was mapped and in 1904 Coaldale became a station on the Tonopah & Goldfield Railroad. But the town failed as a mining promotion and few lots were sold in the townsite. In 1911 there was a brief revival and some production of coal continued into 1913. The 1910 census showed a population of less than 50. [JG]

61. COBRE. Located in Elko County, 33 miles E of Wells. A railroad junction settlement, the northern terminus of the Nevada Northern Railroad, where it connected with the Southern Pacific. The Nevada Northern was built by Nevada Consolidated Copper Company and was completed in 1908. This short line railroad ran from Ely to Cobre, carrying both passengers and freight, but mostly ore from the copper mines in the Ely Mining District. The large building in the center of this view is the depot. [RONL]

62.   COLUMBIA. Located in Esmeralda County, 1 mile N of Goldfield. "Columbia, looking West, by Welch & Tune, Goldfield, Nev." Card is dated June 14, 1908. Columbia was a suburb of Goldfield, but a town in its own right, with many stores, professional offices, hotels, restaurants, post office, ice house, saloons and bank. In 1908 Columbia had a population of 1,500. The large structure at top center is the Combination Mill, complete with a railroad spur line for moving ore cars to and from the mill. The depot for the Tonopah & Goldfield and Bullfrog and Goldfield railroads was located in Columbia. [RG]

63. CONTACT. Located in Elko County, 50 miles N of Wells. A view of the town center, *circa* 1915, when copper mining had reached its peak here. The town had a newspaper, the *Contact Miner*, hotel, stores, and saloons. When the railroad reached Contact in 1925 there was another period of production, and again, during World War II. Total value of copper mined from 1913 to 1948 is estimated at $183 thousand. [PE]

64. CONTACT. This card is a promotion piece for the townsite of Contact, intended to lure settlers to buy lots in the townsite, *circa* 1924. A copper camp had existed here as early as 1905. During the first World War large amounts of copper were shipped. With the completion in 1925 of the Oregon Short Line Railroad into Contact, production resumed and electric power was brought to this remote region in anticipation of a boom. But depressed copper prices and the Great Depression punctured the boom, and hopes for Contact becoming the "largest city in Nevada" came to nothing. [RONL]

65. COPPER BASIN. Located in Lander County, 10 miles SW of Battle Mountain. Ore values were first discovered here in 1864. But it was not until 1897 when the Glasgow & Western Mining Company entered the district that the camp of Copper Basin was created. Low-grade copper was mined, but the district has also produced small amounts of gold, silver, turquoise, and lead. Production peaked during World War I, but the ground has been worked intermittently since. There was a post office here from May 3, 1906 to November 15, 1906. Date of this card is *circa* 1910. [DOUG]

66. COPPER FLAT. Located in White Pine County, 5.5 miles NW of Ely. A view of the open pit at Copper Flat (later known as Ruth) by C. D. Gallagher, dated 1909. This view shows the extensive operations of Nevada Consolidated Copper Company, which had acquired the Copper Flat property in 1905. Shortly after 1900, with the rising development of the electrical industry and the telephone, copper became an important industrial metal and was in great demand. It was needed for motor windings, wiring in homes and factories, for electric and telephone lines. Consumption of the metal rose rapidly, and Nevada was one of the largest suppliers. [PE]

67. COPPER FLAT. This photo shows an ore train leaving the open pit, bound for the concentrator plant at McGill. These two views show the depth the open pit had reached in 1909. As mining continued through the years the pit was expanded and deepened, eventually reaching a depth of nearly 1,000 feet. [PE]

68. CUPRITE. Located in Esmeralda County, 13 miles S of Goldfield. Cuprite is red copper oxide, almost pure copper, and the camp was so named in 1902 when copper ore was found here. But the deposits were quickly worked out. The dwelling pictured here is typical of shelters early prospectors lived in. Using whatever materials were available, some put up shelters made out of barrels, bottles, and even tin cans. Cuprite was a station on the Bullfrog & Goldfield Railroad, and a supply point for the nearby mining camps of Hornsilver, Bonnie Clare and Lida. [RONL]

69. DARROUGHS HOT SPRINGS. Located in Nye County, 23 miles NW of Manhattan. Photo shows the original stone building built in 1863 as a station for stage and mail routes. In 1908, it was expanded into a small hotel and bar. To the left of the building is the hot springs pool, from which steam can be seen rising. This is the first settlement in Big Smoky Valley, and the springs are mentioned in Fremont's 1845 *Report* . The place was named for James T. Darrough, who settled here in the 1880's. [RG]

70. DAYTON. Located in Lyon County, 12 miles NE of Carson City. Card is dated 1908. At this time Dayton was the county seat but in 1909 the courthouse burned to the ground. Yerington was then chosen as the new county seat and the new courthouse built there because of the revenues produced by the copper mines at nearby Mason and Ludwig. The town was named in honor of John Day, who surveyed the townsite, and who later became Surveyor General of Nevada, 1868-1874. [ROGL]

71. DAYTON. The Nevada Reduction Works Mill was located at Rock Point, near Dayton, on the Carson River. Since the early 1860's, ore from the Comstock had been milled here, first in a primitive mill, then at the C. C. Stevenson Mill, and later, after substantial improvements were made, by Nevada Reduction. In May, 1909 the mill pictured here was completely destroyed by fire. [PE]

72. DAYTON. A group of locals pose for the camera in front of the historic Odeon Hall, *circa* 1911. The building was damaged in the fire of 1870 but was rebuilt by the Odd Fellows as their lodge and meeting hall. In later years it was used for a grocery store and meat market, saloon, and town meeting hall. Dances were held in the upstairs portion of the building. In 1960 it was used in filming several interior scenes for John Huston's movie, *The Misfits*, starring Marilyn Monroe, Clark Gable, and Montgomery Clift. [PE]

73. DEETH. Located in Elko County, 35 miles E of Elko. A panorama of Deeth in 1908, several years before the fire of 1915 which destroyed much of the town, photographed by Atherton & Son, of Elko. A prolonged drought struck the area soon after the fire, lasting several years. Water supplies dried up. Crops were destroyed by infestations of crickets and rabbits. With four years of little or no rain and the mountain snow-pack gone, reservoirs dried up, and farmers abandoned their land as taxes became delinquent. [NHS]

74.   DEETH. The Deeth Mercantile Company was owned by Verrill Black and W. H. Smiley. An agricultural community with a population of 250 in 1914, the town was on the line of the Western Pacific and Southern Pacific railroads. Most of the people were active in some form of agriculture, such as stockman, dairyman, orchardist, stock breeding, poultry farming, etc. In 1915 a fire destroyed most of Deeth, from which it never completely recovered. [RONL]

75. DELAMAR. Located in Lincoln County, 37 miles SW of Pioche. Date of this card is *circa* 1906, when the mines at Delamar were still producing significant amounts of gold. Gold was first discovered here in 1890, and several small camps—Ferguson, Helene, and Golden City— sprang up in the district. In 1893 John De Lamar bought up most of the claims and founded the town of Delamar. He brought the Delamar Mine into production and built a 50-ton mill. The ore in the district contained much silica dust, which affected the lungs of miners and those who worked in the mills, often fatally. By 1897 Delamar had 3,000 population. But in 1900 a fire destroyed much of the town, and by 1909 most of the mines had closed. [JJ]

76. DERBY. Located in Washoe County, 27 miles E of Reno. In 1906 Derby was a station on the Southern Pacific Railroad. There was a stamp mill here in 1908, owned by C. F. Kolster. Population at this time was 50. Derby was a construction camp for workers on the Truckee-Carson Reclamation Project, which had begun work on dams and irrigation canals in 1901. The workers were a rowdy bunch when they were not working and the camp became notorious for its lawlessness. Shown here is the Derby Hotel, which was also the office for the local stage line. Card is dated 1910, postmarked Derby. The post office was closed in 1922. [JG]

77. DIAMONDFIELD. Located in Esmeralda County, 4 miles NE of Goldfield. A view of Main Street, *circa* 1907. The town was more of a promotion than a viable mining camp, though the Highland Mine had been worked earlier, then abandoned. Diamondfield Jack Davis, founder of the town, and one of the more colorful characters associated with Nevada's twentieth-century mining boom, was sometimes seen in the company of George Wingfield and Governor John Sparks. He gained wealth and fame during the Goldfield excitement, but afterward is found drifting around the West, his fortune gone. He tried a comeback in mining stocks at Divide, and later, at Goodsprings, but failed. He died in Las Vegas in 1949, where he is said to have worked as a shill for a casino, after being struck down by a taxi on Glitter Gulch. [NHS]

78. DIAMONDFIELD. This photo shows an auto parked on Main Street in front of "The Limit," a saloon and restaurant. No diamonds were ever found at Diamondfield. The place got its name from Diamondfield Jack Davis, who first promoted the town in 1903. He had come from Idaho, convicted of murder, where he had been pardoned at the very last minute by the Governor, standing on the gallows, a noose around his neck. But this is perhaps a melodramatic version told by Davis himself, who relished his reputation as a badman. The town reached its peak in 1904 but could not compete with the excitement at nearby Goldfield. [RG]

79. DIAMONDFIELD. This makeshift schoolhouse was typical of small mining camps—and in keeping with their ephemeral existence—a wood-frame building on a stone foundation, and little else. In 1905 the camp had a population of some 200, and a post office had opened in 1904. Note the man at right holding a camera. [ROGL]

80. DIVIDE. Located in Esmeralda County, 5 miles S of Tonopah. Gold outcroppings were first found here in 1901, but the discovery was eclipsed by the excitement at Tonopah. The place revived in 1908, when this photo card was made by N. E. Johnson. The view shows Divide situated on the slopes of Gold Mountain, with numerous buildings, mine headframes, and roads. But it was not until 1917 that a real boom developed, when rich silver ore was located. A modest rush developed, and a much larger stock pro-motion followed. Diamondfield Jack Davis was one of many who arrived here and engaged in stock pro-motion. Claims were staked out in all directions. But by the end of 1919, Divide was virtually abandoned except for an occasional prospect. [PE]

81. EASTGATE. Located in Churchill County, 61 miles SE of Fallon. This was a station on the overland route in the early days, on the west slope of the Desatoya Range near the Lander County line, and known as Eastgate Station. Nearby was the Eastgate Mining District, where a gold strike occurred in 1906. A townsite was laid out, lots sold, and a camp with a hotel and several stores followed. But there were no subsequent discoveries and the town died a quick death. The view on this card is Eastgate Station, as it appeared in 1911. [JG]

82. EDGEMONT. Located in Elko County, 92 miles NNW of Elko. Freely translated, Edgemont means "on the edge of the mountain," in this case on the steep slopes of the Bull Run Mountains in the Aura Mining District. In 1913 several mines were active here, with six miles of underground workings, a cross-cut tunnel 1,500 feet below the surface, an aerial tramway, and the mill shown here. The district produced about $1 million in gold. But avalanches were a constant menace. In 1906 a quartz mill was destroyed. Then in the winter of 1917 during a heavy snow storm an avalanche swept away the mill shown here, and a boarding house and assay office. [GS]

83. ELKO. County seat of Elko County. A view of Commercial Street, showing the Reinhart Store, Henderson Bank, John Russell Hardware Store, etc. The Reinhart family operated stores in Winnemucca, Elko, Eureka, and Tuscarora, and first began business in Nevada in 1868, in Winnemucca. Elko was also a supply center for a number of mining camps in the county and surrounding area: Gold Circle, Jarbidge, Contact, Sprucemont, and Bullion. Date of this card is *circa* 1913. [JG]

84. ELKO. Construction of the courthouse in Elko was commenced in 1910, when the old court house, built in 1869 on the same site at the corner of Sixth and Idaho Streets, was demolished. Cost of the new courthouse was $150,000, a considerable sum at the time. The building in the foreground is the Presbyterian Church, built at a cost of $20,000, and completed in 1911. Between the church and the courthouse is the Y.M.C.A., completed the same year. [RG]

85. ELKO. This card is dated February 21, 1909, and shows the Chinese Joss House on Chinese New Year. Note the display of flags and banners. Elko was on the line of the old Central Pacific Railroad which had imported many Chinese workers, and many Chinese stayed on in the area after the railroad was completed. Nearly every railroad town had a small Chinese community. Many settled in mining camps and took up mining, as in Tuscarora, where there was a large Chinese community. Others found work on ranches, and others operated small shops selling Chinese goods. [RONL]

86. ELKO. The Elko Grammar School was completely destroyed by fire on December 24, 1918. No one was in the building at the time. School had been closed for two months because of the nationwide influenza epidemic. Fire fighters, whose coats and faces were covered with ice because of the freezing cold, had to be treated for frostbite despite intense heat from the fire. Cause of the fire was attributed to a defective flue in the furnace room. The school had been built in 1908 at a cost of $55,000. [ROGL]

87. ELKO HOT SPRINGS. Located in Elko County, 2 miles S of Elko. The springs had originally been a watering place for travelers on the old emigrant trail. In 1869 the property was developed into a spa and hotel known as White Sulphur Hot Springs. Two fires before 1900 burned the hotel to the ground each time. In 1900 Mrs. J. J. Garrecht, proprietress, who had barely escaped the fire in 1899 with her life, rebuilt the hotel—this time of fireproof brick. The vehicle shown here provided free transportation for guests from the railroad depot to the hotel. [PE]

88. ELLENDALE. Located in Nye County, 30 miles E of Tonopah. Gold was discovered here in the spring of 1909 by Ellen Clifford. She and her husband, James Clifford, both of Tonopah, had gone on a prospecting trip into the desert in their automobile. Mrs. Clifford struck a boulder with her pick and exposed a piece of gold leaf. After some weeks they located the ledge from which the float had come. The leaf gold had been formed from the slow crystallization of gold more typical of the Mother Lode Region of California, and very rare in Nevada. Over a few weeks time the Cliffords gathered sixty sacks of leaf gold, each sack worth $1,000. Later, when dynamite was used to sink a shaft, the shot blew all the fragile leaf gold into fragments, scattering it over the desert. [NHS]

89. ELLENDALE. A Fourth of July celebration at Ellendale, 1909. When word of the discovery got out, hundreds crowded into Ellendale. Town lots were auctioned off at incredible prices. There was even talk of building a railroad line from Tonopah. Leases changed hands at escalating prices. But the bright hopes for Ellendale were not to be realized. The shallow deposits were quickly worked out. No ore or veins at depth were found. Inside a year most of the hopefuls had moved on to the next boomtown, or back to Tonopah. This is a remarkable pair of photo cards, considering how short-lived was Ellendale . [NHS]

90. ELY. County seat of White Pine County. A photo card made by C. D. Gallagher of Ely, *circa* 1910. As early as 1867 gold deposits were worked in the area. But it was not until 1887, when Ely was made a county seat that a town took shape. After 1900, extensive copper deposits were found, and in 1906 the Nevada Northern Railroad from Ely to Cobre was completed. By 1907 there were some 5,000 people here, many of them miners. Several large copper companies were organized: Nevada Consolidated Copper, Consolidated Copper Mines, Steptoe Valley Mining & Smelting, and copper production commenced on a large scale. [RG]

91. ELY. View shows a crowd gathered for a Labor Day celebration, with preparations underway for a drilling contest. By 1910 the population had increased 279 percent over the census of 1900, three times as great as the average growth of Nevada. The price of real estate skyrocketed. By 1910 Ely had a modern water system, cement sidewalks, electric power, schools, telephone system, and county office buildings. It had the largest payroll of any mining town in Nevada. As the copper boom continued, even more new ore bodies were discovered, and from 1908-1940 the Nevada Consolidated Copper Company produced over $316 million, making it second only to the Comstock Lode in total production. [RG]

92. ELY. The route of the New York to Paris Around the World Automobile Race in 1908 took the drivers and their machines through Nevada. Here an American car in the race stops at Ely, gathering a large crowd of onlookers. The driver appears at the rear of the car, turning to face the camera, wearing a heavy coat with a fur collar, cap and driving goggles. There are also photo cards showing the race cars in Tonopah and Goldfield. The race was won by a Thomas Flyer, now in the National Automobile Museum, Reno. [PE]

93. ELY. Games were a popular form of entertainment among the North American Indians. Some tribes had their own games of chance, and the Shoshone were no exception. Here a group of Shoshone women seated around a blanket are playing a game of chance. Gambling had long been a part of the Shoshone and Paiute cultures. When archaeological digs were made at Lost City and Paiute Cave in 1925, some 50 miles northeast of Las Vegas, among the artifacts found in ancient graves were primitive gaming dice made of animal bone. [PE]

94. EMPIRE. Located in Ormsby County, 3 miles E of Carson City. Originally known as Empire City in the early Comstock period, and located on the Carson River, Empire dates back to territorial days. It was a station on the Virginia & Truckee Railroad. In its heyday—between 1865 and 1875—several quartz mills were in operation, processing ores from the Comstock. At the peak of its prosperity, some 700 people lived here. With the decline of the Comstock, Empire also declined. Some 150 people lived here in 1907. Because of its proximity to the Carson River, Empire was subject to spring flooding, as shown in this 1907 view. [JG]

95. EUREKA. County seat of Eureka County, 70 miles E of Austin. This is a panorama view, *circa* 1908, by an anonymous photographer. The town had its beginnings much earlier, about 1870, and for a time was second in population and mining wealth only to Virginia City. The discovery of rich silver ore at Ruby Hill (operated by the Eureka Consolidated Mining Company), and the completion of the Eureka and Palisade Railroad brought prosperity and fame to the town. In 1880 the population was 7,000. There were stores of all descriptions, two theaters, three hotels, two daily newspapers, banks, schools, doctors and lawyers. [RONL]

96. EUREKA. A Labor Day parade, *circa* 1909, complete with a brass band. By this time the population had declined to around 1,000. The Eureka Consolidated and the Richmond—the two principal mines in the district—had suspended operations in 1891 due to expensive litigation and a drop in the price of silver. Before closing down, these two mines had produced $33 million in silver. The output of the entire district of over 400 mines had amounted to $200 million, of which $44 million was paid out in dividends to stockholders and owners. [RONL]

97. EUREKA. The Eureka baseball team poses for a photograph before boarding a Eureka and Palisade train for a baseball game, *circa* 1912. [PE]

98. EUREKA. View shows Main Street in the early 1920's, when the population had declined to a mere 500. It was at this time the southern terminus of the Eureka and Palisade Railroad, with connections at Palisade to the Southern Pacific and Western Pacific railroads. Interest in mineral prospecting had shifted from gold and silver to lead, copper, antimony, and zinc. In 1915, a local business directory listed more entries for people engaged in livestock and ranching than mining. [NHS]

99. FAIRVIEW. Located in Churchill County, 42 miles ESE of Fallon. A stagecoach pauses on Fairview's Main Street, *circa* 1907. The town boomed rapidly and by the spring of 1906 some 2,000 people had arrived here. Lots on Main Street sold for $100 a front foot. Soon there was a newspaper, hotel, bank, post office, and saloons. From 1906-1910 the mines were worked by lease arrangements, and through this method considerable mining was done and capital invested. After 1917, when the Nevada Hills Mining Company suspended operations, leasers continued to work the district for another two years. But by 1920 only a few people remained in Fairview. [PE]

100. FAIRVIEW. A view of the Nevada Hills Mining Company property, issued by the Nevada Post Card Company. In the beginning, most of the prospects were worked by leasers, one of whom was Henry Curtis Morris, author of two books on his Nevada mining experiences: *Desert Gold and Total Prospecting*, 1955, and *The Mining West at the Turn of the Century*, 1962. Both books contain valuable information on Fairview and Wonder. [RG]

101. FAIRVIEW. The Nevada Hills Mine commenced operations in 1911 and was owned by George Wingfield and associates, of Reno. A 20-stamp mill was built, and a mining journal of the day called it one of the finest mills in the world. The mill was operated by a large electric power plant which also generated enough electricity for the entire town. The mine produced some $10 million in gold and silver until 1917, when veins were exhausted. This card was published by the Nevada Post Card Company, of Goldfield, a companion to the card above, and is distinguished by a green tint. [RG]

102. FALLON. County seat of Churchill County, 68 miles E of Reno. On May 14, 1910, a fire swept through the business district of Fallon. It lasted only one hour and fifteen minutes, but the damage was considerable. When the smoke cleared, it was discovered sixteen business establishments had been burned out, with losses estimated at $75,000. It took many days to sort through the rubble and clear away the debris. A loss of such magnitude would have spelled the end for many small mining camps, but Fallon's wealth was in farm lands and agriculture, and so the merchants quickly rebuilt. The sign at the upper left on the stone building advertises stage service to Rawhide, Fairview and Wonder. [RG]

103.   FALLON. This card shows a group posed for a photograph in front of the Fallon depot, *circa* 1910. The town is a station on a branch line of the Southern Pacific Railroad. In 1907 the Southern Pacific built a branch line from Hazen to Fallon, connecting it with the Nevada & California Railroad. Later that year there was talk of building a line from Fallon to Fairview and Wonder, via Stillwater and Hercules, but nothing came of the project. [RONL]

104. FALLON. Members of the Fallon baseball team, *circa* 1911, at Lovelock for a league game. Caption at bottom reads: "Fallon team at Lovelock. Osborn Photo." [PE]

Mining supplies for Farrell, Seven Trough District, Nev.

105. FARRELL. Located in Pershing County, 26 miles NW of Lovelock. Although traces of gold had been found in nearby Stonehouse Canyon as early as the 1860's, Farrell did not come into existence until 1906, when a townsite was laid out. It owed its short life not to any ore deposits, but to the boom psychology caused by the Seven Troughs mining excitement. It was the smallest of the four camps in the district, and the first to fade. During its span of approximately two years, it was mostly a camp of tents, but as can be seen in this view, there were a few wooden buildings. The place was named for William F. Farrell, a local promoter. A post office opened on July 20, 1907, but was discontinued September 30, 1911. [RG]

106. FAY. Located in Lincoln County, 21 miles NW of Modena, Utah. Gold was discovered here in 1900, and several mines and mills operated here until around 1915. A post office opened on September 13, 1900, and was discontinued July 15, 1924. This card is postmarked Fay, dated July 25, 1909. At that time the population was 100. The large white space to the left is a tailing dump. At the top of the view may be seen part of the works of the Horseshoe Mine, the largest in the district, which produced $269,000 from 1900-1902. Fay had telephone connections and daily stage service to Modena, fare $2.00. [JC]

107. FERNLEY. Located in Lyon County, 33 miles E of Reno. This interesting piece of roadside Ameri-cana, *circa* 1928, features a variety of diversions, including swimming in water from a hot springs. The Hot Springs Station was owned by Ike Springer. The town of Fernley was settled in 1905, and was a station on the Southern Pacific Railroad. A post office opened in April, 1908. U. S. Highway 40 is today Interstate 80. [RONL]

108. FLETCHER. Located in Mineral County, 18 miles SW of Hawthorne. Date of card is May 4, 1911 and shows the old stage stop and way station on the Lucky Boy Grade. The station was built in the 1880's when there was considerable traffic between Bodie and Hawthorne. A post office was established here in October, 1883 and after April, 1884 transferred to Hawthorne and Lucky Boy. [PE]

109. FORT McDERMITT. Located in Humboldt County, 70 miles N of Winnemucca, and 5 miles E of the town of McDermitt. The fort was established in the 1860's to protect travelers on the route from Virginia City to Idaho from Indian raiding parties. In later years the fort became an Indian Reservation, using its reconstructed buildings as a community center. In 1911, about the time this photograph was taken, there were 313 Indians living there, including 103 children, who attended the local reservation school. [GS]

110. GARDNERVILLE. Located in Douglas County, 22 miles S of Carson City. The town was founded by Lawrence Gilmore, who located a hotel on the site. Gilmore named the town for John M. Gardner, a pioneer rancher in the area. It remained a trading center for ranches in the area until 1885, when the needs of miners in outlying districts brought about the establishment of stores. The town had several hotels, livery stables, churches, a county high school, and several professional people. This photo is dated August 6, 1911 and shows a general merchandise store, post office, saloon, barber shop, and hotel. [RG]

111. GARDNERVILLE. View shows a freighting wagon and team hauling a load of sacked produce. Note the wagon works and blacksmith shop at right, with the quaint sign. The town is located in an excellent agricultural district, most of the land under irrigation. In 1910 Gardnerville was the largest town in Douglas County, with a population of 1,000. When the county seat was moved from Genoa, Gardnerville lost out to Minden in a bid to become the new county seat. [RONL]

112. GARDNERVILLE. A cattle drive down Main Street, leaving a cloud of dust in its wake. During late spring, when forage became scarce at the lower range elevations, it was customary to drive cattle to higher pastures where grass was more plentiful. From Gardnerville and Minden, cattle were driven to a summer range in the Sierra Nevada, in the vicinity of Woodfords, near Lake Tahoe. [PE]

113. GENOA. Located in Douglas County, 15 miles SW of Carson City. The building shown here is the fort and trading post known as Old Mormon Station, originally built in 1850-51. It was destroyed by fire in 1911. Genoa is the oldest settlement in Nevada, founded by Mormons, and originally a part of Utah Territory. The first newspaper printed in Nevada, *The Daily Territorial Enterprise*, commenced publication here on December 18, 1858. The first effort to create Nevada Territory occurred here in 1857, when residents along the eastern Sierra convened to petition Congress. But it was not until 1861 that President Abraham Lincoln officially created Nevada Territory. [GS]

114. GENOA. Organized in 1869, the Genoa Lodge had approximately 50 members when this photograph was taken, *circa* 1906. The brick building in front of which the members are assembled is the I.O.O.F. Hall in Genoa. The first I.O.O.F. Lodge in Nevada was organized in 1861 at Virginia City. In 1867, the Grand Lodge of Nevada was formed, comprised of ten local lodges around the state. By 1913 there were twenty-five active lodges, with a membership of over 1,700. [DOUG]

115. GERLACH. Located in Washoe County, 125 miles NE of Reno. The town was settled in 1906 and was named for the Gerlach Land & Cattle Company. It was on the main line of the Western Pacific Railroad. This card is *circa* 1912 when the town had a population of 250. It was a shipping point for many small communities and ranches in the area. South of Gerlach, some 12 miles distant, was the Gerlach Mining District, which produced considerable quantities of gypsum. The town supported four general merchandise stores and several saloons. [RONL]

116. GERLACH. Date of this card is *circa* 1910 and shows the embryonic townsite at the time gypsum deposits were discovered in the district, and when the Western Pacific Railroad was building its main line through the township. The post office was established October 27, 1909 and shared space with the local general merchandise store. [PE]

117. GILBERT. Located in Esmeralda County, 25 miles W of Tonopah. An early photograph of Gilbert, before the boom had reached its peak. The richest properties were owned by the Gilbert brothers, who sent ore shipments by truck into Tonopah under armed guard. The Tonopah & Goldfield Railroad proposed building a spur line into Gilbert, but the mines soon became worked out and the route was never surveyed. [ROGL]

118. GLENBROOK. Located in Douglas County, 22 miles SW of Carson City. This card is from an early photograph, showing a group enjoying their vacation at the Lakeshore House. Glenbrook was a popular resort in the late nineteenth-century, situated in a sheltered cove on the northeastern shore of Lake Tahoe. In the mid-1870's it had been a busy lumber camp, supplying timber for the Comstock mines. In 1876 the Lake Tahoe Narrow Gauge Railroad was built from Glenbrook to the eastern summit of the Sierra Nevada for moving timber to a flume, where it then traveled downslope to Carson City. [NHS]

119. GOLCONDA. Located in Humboldt County, 16 miles E of Winnemucca. Originally a station on the Central Pacific Railroad in 1868, the town of Golconda became a mining center in 1896 when Scottish investors purchased the Adelaide Mine, built a large smelter, and financed the Golconda & Adelaide Railroad. Some 120 men were employed at the mine and smelter. Prospects for Golconda looked bright. This photo card, dated July, 1910 shows the Golconda Mercantile & Banking Company, owned by Fred W. Noble, at left. The large brick building is one of six hotels built around 1900. At right is the Opera Star Bar & Cafe. In 1899 the Golconda & Adelaide Railroad was completed. However, the Adelaide Mine failed as a profitable venture. The mine, smelter, and railroad were eventually abandoned. By 1916 the smelter and railroad had been dismantled, and Golconda's boom days were over. [RG]

Golconda Hot Springs Hotel, Golconda, Nev.

120. GOLCONDA HOT SPRINGS. Located in Humboldt County, 17 miles E of Winnemucca. In 1908 the Hot Springs Hotel was owned and operated by Eugene L. Dutertre. As the town of Golconda was a station on the Western Pacific and Southern Pacific railroads, health-seekers from all over the nation found the hot mineral springs easy of access. The hotel employed a trained staff, offered comfortable lodging and surroundings. The springs were advertised as possessing healing properties for a variety of ailments. [RONL]

121. GOLD BAR. Located in Nye County, approximately 4 miles NW of Rhyolite. Photograph by A. E. Holt of Rhyolite, dated November, 1905. This early view of Gold Bar shows a camp of tents before the boom of 1907 occurred. The camp owed its existence to the discovery of the Gold Bar Mine in August, 1904 by Benny Hazeltine. The mine was located about three miles due north of the Original Bullfrog Mine, discovered by "Shorty" Harris and Eddie Cross in August, 1904. [NHS]

122. GOLD BAR. "Camp at Gold Bar and Homestake," by A. E. Holt of Rhyolite. A later view of the camp than shown on the preceding card, which shows a number of wooden buildings spread over the townsite. Ore from the Gold Bar Mine was shipped on the Las Vegas & Tonopah Railroad from a siding at Gold Bar switch, about 1.2 miles west of the camp. There was a hotel here, several saloons, and a post office served the camp from May 30, 1907 until July 15, 1909. After 1909 the camp was abandoned and it is not listed in the 1910 census. [NHS]

123. GOLD CIRCLE. Located in Elko County, 62 miles WNW of Elko. There was a rush of considerable proportions here in 1907-08 when gold was discovered in nearby canyons. Known as Gold Circle in 1907 (until November 16) because the mines in the district formed a circle around the camp. The name was changed to Midas [q.v.] at the request of the U. S. Post Office to avoid confusion with the many towns and camps in Nevada whose names began with the word "gold." Postal service began on November 16, 1907 using the new name of "Midas." [PE]

124. GOLDFIELD. County seat of Esmeralda County, 25 miles S of Tonopah. In the spring and summer of 1903 only a few prospectors were at Goldfield, which was still called "Grandpa," or "Gran Pah" (its original name) by its discoverers. This is one of the earliest photographs extant of Goldfield, showing a small grouping of tents, one small wood-frame building, and another being framed by three men in the foreground. In those early days the true value of the ground was not known, as early assays had not been particularly encouraging. As a result, claims changed hands frequently. In late October, 1903, thirty-six of the original Goldfielders met to form the Goldfield Mining District, name the town "Goldfield" (after its namesake in Colorado), and to write its mining laws. [PE]

125. GOLDFIELD. During the height of its fame, the streets of Goldfield hummed with activity. Saloons and dance halls were open through the night, as was the Goldfield Stock Exchange. This photo was made in 1909 when the richest ground had been staked. George Wingfield, a former faro dealer from Tonopah, gained control of the richest mines with a loan from eastern financier Bernard Baruch. Wingfield, together with his business partner George Nixon, merged these properties into what became Goldfield Consolidated, and through this merger exercised considerable control over Goldfield mining stocks, many of which doubled and tripled in price before and after the merger mania. [MK]

126. GOLDFIELD. An excellent photograph of prospectors about to leave for the desert, taken by Welch & Tune, Goldfield photographers. These photographers issued a number of real photo post cards of Goldfield and the surrounding area. Card is postmarked Goldfield, dated August 3, 1907. Burros were still a common means of packing supplies. Note how their loads have been carefully lashed with ropes. To some extent automobiles had replaced burros by 1907 but burros could go places autos could not and were not susceptible to mechanical breakdowns. [RG]

127. GOLDFIELD. "Merchants Hotel. Welch & Tune, Goldfield, Nev." Card is dated May 28, 1908. More money is said to have passed over the gaming tables in Goldfield than in any other activity, except for stock promotions. Casinos operated around the clock. Gold and silver coins served as chips. The game at right is craps; note the primitive layout on the table, unlike today's crap tables. The game at lower left is faro, the most popular game of that time, and with the best odds for the player. Above the faro table is a roulette wheel. Note the complete absence of slot machines. Of interest in this photo is the woman standing near the door, for any respectable lady did not generally frequent saloons and casinos in that day and age, although some saloons had private entrances and rooms for ladies. Gambling was prohibited by law in Nevada on October 1, 1910. It was again legalized in 1931. [CS]

128. GOLDFIELD. A group of revelers at a Goldfield dance hall, *circa* 1907. Note that some of the dancers are masked, suggesting a masked ball. Note the sign, partly obscured in the back ground, which reads: "This is strictly a union house." Goldfield was very much a pro-union town and the labor troubles that occurred in 1906-07 play an important part in Goldfield's history. But the town also had its merrier side. There were several theaters, elegant restaurants and social clubs, casinos, baseball clubs, boxing, and amateur horseracing. [RG]

129. GOLDFIELD. This card, issued to promote the Nelson-Gans fight, looks like a modern post card, but in fact is 1906. Special trains came from Chicago and San Francisco for the fight, which was promoted by Tex Rickard. The purse of $30 thousand (in $20 gold pieces) was on display in a window of the John S. Cooke Bank in Goldfield a week before the fight. The sender of this card has written: "What a hot town this will be on 9/3/06. Started already." The fight went forty-two rounds and lasted almost three hours. Gans won on a foul and was awarded the purse. The event brought considerable money into Goldfield and did much to publicize the town all over the nation. [RONL]

130. GOLDFIELD. Federal troops were sent into Goldfield on December 6, 1907 by President Theodore Roosevelt at the request of Governor John Sparks (and through the instigation of George Wingfield) to break a strike called by the I. W. W. (Wobblies) and the Western Federation of Miners. Wingfield had gained control of the richest mines at this time and had merged them into Goldfield Consolidated. The unions collapsed in the face of federal troop intervention on April 3, 1908, after holding out for four months. [PE]

131. GOLDFIELD. Elinor Glyn's visit to Goldfield and Rawhide in 1905 attracted nation-wide
publicity. Her sensational novel, *Three Weeks*, had
recently been suppressed in puritanical circles
(thereby guaranteeing its success) and when local
promoters Nat Goodwin and George
Graham Rice got word she might be interested in
seeing first-hand a genuine wild west town,
they saw a publicity opportunity not to be missed.
Elinor was treated to a variety of staged saloon
brawls and fake shoot-outs. The message on card
reads: "The Invincible Elinor has been in Goldfield for one week (not 3) and this is a pretty
good picture of her. She's a good one." She went
to Hollywood in the 1920's and worked for Para-
mount and Metro as a screenwriter, her specialty
being romance films. She had considerable influ-
ence on developing star personalities, creating a
particular mystique to suit a particular star. She
chose Clara Bow as the "It" girl. [RG]

132. GOLD HILL. Located in Storey County, 3/4 mile S of Virginia City. This view of Gold Hill
was taken from an early photograph, *circa* 1875, showing the town at the height of its prosperity. Tracks
and trestle of the Virginia & Truckee Railroad can be seen at bottom left. Population at this time was
8,500 and the town had fire companies, schools, churches, fraternal organizations, street lamps, a water
company, and the famous newspaper, *The Gold Hill News*, edited by Alf Doten. [RG]

133. GOLD HILL. Date of this card is *circa* 1909. The tall spire of the Catholic Church can be seen at right. The business district is above the mine dump at center. Population at this time was 500. Mines in the lower Comstock were still being worked for low-grade ores, chiefly the Overman, Yellow Jacket, and Confidence. [RONL]

134. GOLD HILL. Caption on card reads: "Yellow Jacket Mill, Gold Hill, Nev." The Yellow Jacket Mine and Mill were still in operation in 1910, processing low-grade ores. In the early days of the Comstock it was one of the great bonanza mines, rich in gold and silver. A disastrous fire occurred on April 24, 1869 when underground timbering caught fire and forty-five miners lost their lives. By 1876 the Yellow Jacket had produced over $10 million. [PE]

135. GOLD HILL. The Belcher Mine was at the lower end of the Comstock Lode. It was originally owned by William C. Ralston, president of the Bank of California. Between 1871 and 1881 the mine produced some $36 million in silver and gold, but became increasingly difficult to work because of intense heat as miners worked at ever-lower depths. Matters improved when the Sutro Tunnel was completed, which allowed for ventilation and drainage. But in 1882, after ore values had begun to decline, an immense flow of hot water was struck and all underground workings were flooded. [RG]

136. GOLD REEF. Located in Esmeralda County, 6 miles SSE of Tonopah. Reports of a gold strike here in 1909 caused a brief flurry of excitement, but it quickly faded. Gold Reef was never more than a few tents and a handful of prospectors and promoters. This photograph by E. W. Smith of Tonopah looks suspiciously like a promotion piece. One would hardly venture out into the desert with a burro train dressed as three of these men are, wearing suits, neckties, and dress shoes. [PE]

137. GOODSPRINGS. Located in Clark County, 34 miles SW of Las Vegas. A panorama view, *circa* 1916 showing buildings of the Yellow Pine Mining Company at left and the Fayle Hotel at lower right center. Although silver and lead deposits had been discovered here as early as 1868, there was no permanent settlement until 1888. When the Keystone Mine struck gold ore in 1892, and when the Nevada Southern Railroad was built into Manvel, California (45 miles to the south), prospects for this mining district improved greatly. Later the Yellow Pine Company was organized, new ore bodies were discovered, chiefly lead and zinc, and the mining company built a narrow gauge line into Goodsprings from Jean. [JG]

138. GOODSPRINGS. The building in this view is the Fayle Hotel with its sweeping porches around both floors, a local landmark in Goodsprings for fifty years, and the hub of its social life. The hotel opened in 1916, offered a dining room and bar to its guests, and occasional weekend dancing. After a long and active life, it burned to the ground in 1966. The flag-raising ceremony shown here was in honor of those young men from Goodsprings who had served in World War I. Mining continued in the Goodsprings District until World War II, and afterward. Total production of the district was $10.4 million through 1940. [JC]

139. GRANITE. Located in Mineral County, 8 miles NW of Schurz. Gold was discovered here in 1908 and a mining district was formed, known as Mountain View and Reservation. The camp was a spin-off of the Rawhide excitement, when prospectors fanned out in every direction searching for new strikes. A small camp of tents, the population of Granite was never larger than 200, though it had a post office from May 5, 1908 to May 15, 1909, and a weekly newspaper written in longhand. The boom was over in less than a year, though occasional leasers continued to work the ground. This rare photograph shows Granite as it appeared in 1909. [DOUG]

140. HAMILTON. Located in White Pine County, 37 miles W of Ely. This photo of Hamilton was taken *circa* 1905 and shows the town in decline. The two-story building at far right with the arched windows is the former Withington Hotel, built in 1869. The facade of the building was faced with stone from a nearby quarry. Earlier in 1868, Hamilton had been the scene of one of the great mining rushes in Nevada, luring almost 10,000 people who hoped for a share of the silver bonanza. In 1869 Hamilton had been made county seat of White Pine County. There were stores of all descriptions, a newspaper, doctors and lawyers, opera houses, breweries, banks, schools, and assay offices. By 1870 the population had declined to 6,800, and a fire in 1873 destroyed several business blocks. [JJ]

141. HAWTHORNE. County seat of Mineral County, 72 miles S of Fallon. Hawthorne was settled in the early 1880's when the Carson & Colorado Railroad made the town its southern terminus and a division point. It was the trading and staging center for a large area, including Bodie, California, where stages ran daily. In 1883 Hawthorne was chosen as county seat of Mineral County over its rival, Aurora. Town improvements included a telephone and water system. This card shows a view of Main Street *circa* 1910, during a parade. The flag at left center and the men in shirt sleeves suggests a Fourth of July celebration. [JC]

142. HAWTHORNE. "Freighting in the Desert. Pulling into Hawthorne, Nev. N. E. Johnson, Photo." Card is dated 1908. Even with competition from the Carson & Colorado Railroad, there was still enough business for the "desert freighters." Mule teams and freighters could haul where the railroad had no track, to new mining camps or distant ranches. Sometimes the only method of transportation for remote mines were the freighters, who would haul rich ore to the nearest railhead. [PE]

143. HAZEN. Located in Churchill County, 45 miles E of Reno. In 1908 Hazen was a town of 150 population and a station on the Southern Pacific Railroad. Originally settled in 1869, it was named for William B. Hazen, a U. S. Army officer and aide to General William T. Sherman. Hazen gained new importance as a railroad center when it became the northern division point for the former Carson & Colorado Railroad, made possible by track laid in 1905 from Tonopah Junction northward to Mound House. [PE]

144. HAZEN. "Red" Wood, robber and possible murderer, was hanged in Hazen around January 1, 1906. He had been run out of Derby where he had operated a notorious and disreputable saloon, and where his partner had disappeared under mysterious circumstances. After an exchange of gunfire, he was captured during an attempted robbery at the Hazen railroad station and locked in jail. During the night the jail was broken into and "Red" was taken out by persons unknown. He was discovered at daylight, hanged from a telegraph pole, as shown in this photograph. The persons responsible for the hanging were never identified. Card is dated January 10, 1906 and the message reads: "This shows some of the scenery of our little city. The 'City Jail' is shown in the background." A note written at top of card reads: "A way they have in 'Hazen' of making *bad* men *good* ." [MK]

145. HAZEN. The Palace Hotel was built in 1908 after a fire had leveled much of the town. Also sharing the same building was the Hazen Trading Co.& General Merchandise, and the post office. A post office was established April 25, 1904 and discontinued June 25, 1979. During the Tonopah, Goldfield boom, Hazen became an important railroad junction for southbound traffic. In later years when traffic declined and the Southern Pacific closed its roundhouse here, Hazen served surrounding ranches as a trading center. [RONL]

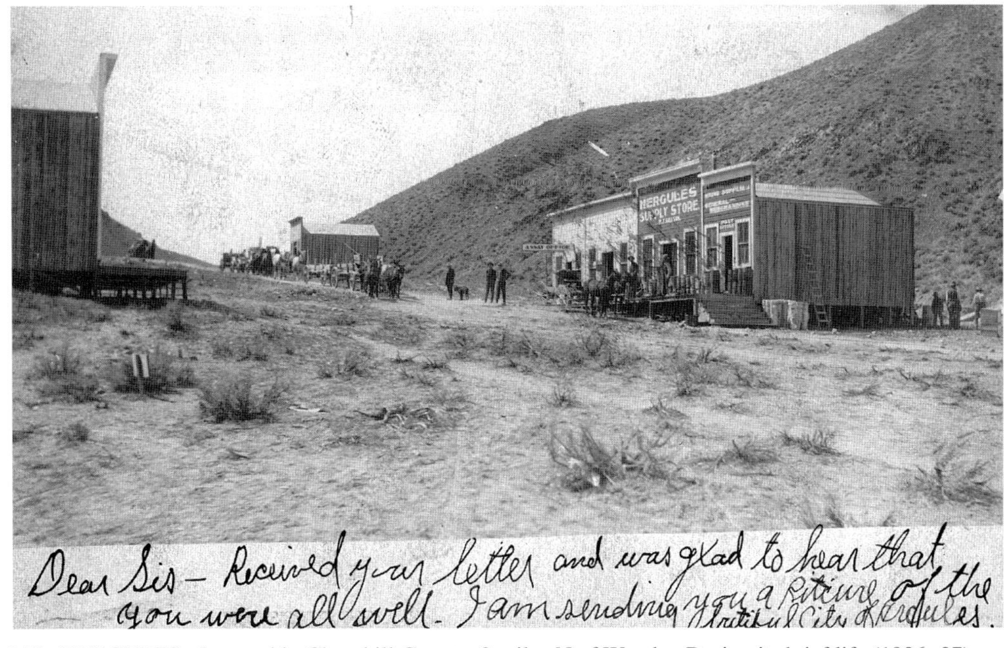

146. HERCULES. Located in Churchill County, 2 miles N of Wonder. During its brief life (1906- 07), Hercules had a newspaper, the *Weekly Miner*, hotel, post office, and saloon. This view shows only a handful of wood-frame buildings, and the camp never grew much beyond what is shown here. When the hotel burned in 1907 the camp went into rapid decline. A post office was opened December 18, 1906 and discontinued October 31, 1908. [JJ]

147. HERCULES. The bar or saloon shown here also appears in the preceding card, in the distance with a line of freight wagons in front. In the Hercules Mining District the three principal mines were the Apex Divide, Hercules Divide, and Giant Divide, all owned by Grant J. Crumley. Electricity for operating the hoists in these mines was brought in over a transmission line from Bishop, California. When the camp was abandoned, the remaining population moved to nearby Wonder. [JJ]

148. HIKO. Located in Lincoln County, on SR 318, 4.6 miles N of its junction with SR 375. Card is dated November 28, 1908 and message reads: "This is a picture of us all at school. There's not many of us but I am learning fast. Willie." Willie is the boy at left of card. Population of Hiko at this time was 100. The word "Hiko" in Shoshone means "white man." The town was first settled in the late 1860's when considerable money was invested in hopes of developing profitable silver mines. Hiko was the county seat until 1871 when it was changed to Pioche. The mines failed to recoup their investment and hopes for Hiko faded. [JG]

149. HILLTOP. Located in Lander County, 18 miles SE of Battle Mountain. Card is postmarked Hilltop and dated 1910. Photo shows a group of children photographed on some special occasion, possibly the Fourth of July. Note the antique baby carriage below the girl holding the flag. A mining district was organized here in 1906 when gold ore was discovered, and a small rush into the area followed. A camp grew up around the mines, with a school, hotel, general merchandise store, and stage office. Six mines were working in 1915. Production continued irregularly through 1924 and the post office was officially closed in 1931. [JG]

150. HORNSILVER. Located in Esmeralda County, 25 miles SW of Goldfield. This settlement was first called Lime Point, then Hornsilver (when rich horn silver ore was discovered in 1908), and then Gold Point in 1932, when a post office was established with that name. One of the signs (at left) in this photo advertises the office of the Fowlie Townsite Company. Apparently this promotion never got off the ground, for no town or townsite by the name of Fowlie, Nevada is listed in Polk's *Nevada Gazetteers*, or in the 1910 U. S. Census. Population of Hornsilver in 1912 was approximately 100. An auto stage ran three times a week to Lida and Goldfield, fare $3.00. [RONL]

151. HORNSILVER. Here assembled on a stage for a photograph are the pioneers of Hornsilver. Harry Wiley, who later became State Senator from Esmeralda County, had been secretary of the Hornsilver Board of Trade in 1907; Pat Burke, proprietor of the Great Western Saloon, had been the town's first mayor; Martin D. Mitchell had been owner of the first mercantile store in town—and others. In 1914 the Apex Mining Group, the Orleans Mine, Silver King Mine, were all still active. Later the Great Western Mine, which yielded low-grade silver and gold, accounted for most of the production from this camp. [RONL]

152. HUMBOLDT HOUSE. Located in Pershing County, 32 miles NE of Lovelock. Built in 1868 by the Central Pacific Railroad, Humboldt House provided a welcome sight to passengers on the overland route after traveling through miles of barren desert. Shade trees and a gushing fountain greeted passengers at the entrance to the dining room. When dining cars were added by the railroad, trains no longer made regular stops here. But the inn continued to serve passengers who traveled by stage, also early automobile travelers. A post office was established in June, 1872 and discontinued November 15, 1909. Card is dated 1909. [PE]

153. IMLAY. Located in Pershing County, 38 miles NE of Lovelock. Named for a civil engineer who surveyed the area in 1908 and selected the site for a new terminal and roundhouse for the Southern Pacific Railroad. The railroad also served several mines to the south of town. The large smokestack and building in the middle distance are the railroad shop facilities and yards. A post office was established in 1908 and several hundred people lived here, most employed by the railroad. Later when shop facilities were moved elsewhere, the town went into decline. [RG]

154. IMLAY. A closer view of the railroad facilities at Imlay, *circa* 1912. The large building in the center of view is the 12-engine roundhouse. Not shown in this view is the employees' clubhouse, a large two-story wooden building with living quarters upstairs, card and billiard rooms on the ground floor. There were also car sheds and repair shops, and a turntable for moving engines into the roundhouse . [PE]

155. INDIAN SPRINGS. Located in Clark County, 44 miles NW of Las Vegas. Originally a station on the Las Vegas & Tonopah Railroad. With the rush to Wahmonie by automobile in 1928, Indian Springs became a "last chance" refueling stop, the only service station for miles in any direction. Sign at right reads: "Wahmonie, 42 miles." Note the truck at right loaded with barrels—either gasoline or water, the gasoline tank truck, and the variety of services offered, including rooms and lunches for the weary traveler. [RM]

156. IONE. Located in Nye County, 64 miles NNW of Tonopah. Silver ore was discovered here in 1863 and the district received favorable mention in the mining press of the day. By the following year Ione had a population of 500. Later, the 20-stamp Knickerbocker Mill was built at a cost of $130,000. Ione was designated county seat of Nye County in 1864. However, the mines never lived up to expectations and in 1867 the county seat was moved to Belmont. This photograph shows Main Street, *circa* 1905 when the town was in decline and the population less than 50. [NHS]

157. JAMESTOWN. Located in Nye County, 39 miles E of Goldfield. Caption on card reads: "Jamestown, Nev. Apr. 08. Altitude 6550." Card is postmarked Goldfield, May 9, 1908. Message reads: "On my way to the new rich strike at Jamestown, Nev. Frank P. Marish, 39 miles east of Gold F." Lettering on wagon at left reads: "Nye County Merc. Co. Goldfield. Tonopah. Manhattan. Rhyolite." View shows a typical desert prospector's outfit. Jamestown never developed much beyond a tent camp, though it did have a post office from June 13, 1908 until August, 1910. [RG]

158. JARBIDGE. Located in Elko County, 96 miles NE of Elko. Gold was discovered in November, 1908 in Jarbidge Canyon, but a rush into the district was slow in starting because of its remote location and the long winters. But by the summer of 1910 some 1,500 people had swarmed into the canyon, excited by reports that millions in gold ore was in plain sight. The reports, of course, were fanciful, and after a particularly severe winter, when prices of goods reached fantastic levels, most of the boomers left. By 1912 the population had dropped to some 250 people. In 1916 the Guggenheim interests had gained control of the best mining properties, built a large mill, and ore was shipped out on a regular basis. [PE]

159. JARBIDGE. In February, 1910 exaggerated reports of millions in gold resulted in a rush of some 1,500 hardy souls into the frozen regions of Jarbidge, including this impractical contraption— a man-drawn sled. Whether this group ever arrived there without busting their backs and with the sled intact is doubtful, given the rough terrain and snowdrifts up to eighteen feet deep. [ROGL]

160. JARBIDGE. This photo card is *circa* 1915 and shows a group of boys on Main Street engaged in a foot race. In 1917 the Elkora Mining Company built a large mill and developed the Flaxico and Hike mining properties. Nevada Power Company built a transmission line seventy-three miles long to bring electricity from a power station on the Snake River in Idaho. Located near the Idaho state line, most supplies were brought in from Twin Falls and Boise, Idaho, and there was regular stage service to Twin Falls. [NHS]

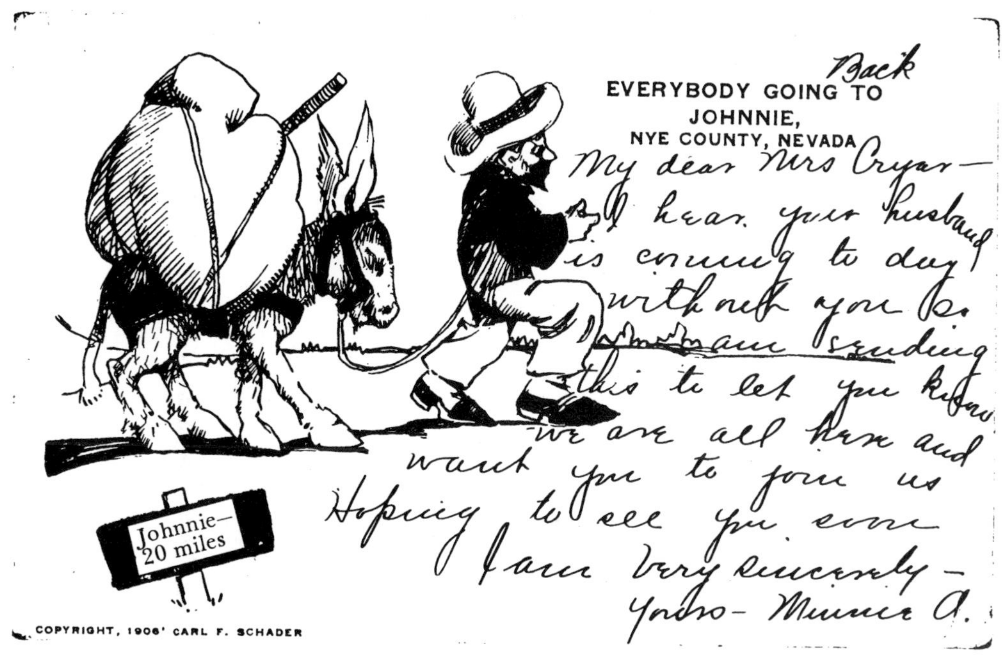

161. JOHNNIE. Located in Nye County, 88 miles NW of Las Vegas. This cartoon post card by
Carl F. Schader is postmarked Johnnie and dated March 7, 1911. Mr. Schader is listed in Polk's
Nevada State Gazetteer, 1907-08, as a mining engineer in Johnnie, and presumably he drew
cartoon post cards in his spare time. A camp formed here when gold was discovered in 1891,
but production on a large scale did not begin until 1898. Bob Montgomery, later of Rhyolite
and Beatty fame, is credited with bringing the Johnnie Mine into production. A townsite was
platted in 1905, lots sold to investors as far away as Los Angeles, and Johnnie was favorably
mentioned in the Tonopah and Rhyolite newspapers. [RM]

162. JUMBO. Located in Washoe County, on the Ophir Grade from Washoe Valley to Virginia City.
With the development of several mines and the construction of a mill, a small camp formed around an
assay office, general merchandise store, saloon and hotel. A post office served the settlement from April
16, 1908 until November 30, 1910. The 1910 census lists a population of 100. This card is dated February
24, 1909. [JG]

163. JUMBO. The Jumbo-Washoe stage, which appears in a state of disuse, was put into service
by the photographer who decided to use it as a prop for this picture, probably taken in Jumbo.
The words "Jumbo" and "Washoe" are partially visible on the coach between the three ladies
standing on the wheels. When it was running, the stage made daily trips to Virginia City and
Washoe. [ROGL]

164. KENNEDY. Located in Pershing County, 56 miles ENE of Lovelock. Mining began here in 1892,
and two years later the camp had a population of 500, a newspaper, *The New Era*, stores, mills, school,
post office, and daily stage service to Lovelock. The Imperial Mine was the largest producer in the district
in 1900 and was purchased by the Gold Note Mining & Milling Company in 1906. The camp suffered
severe damage in an earthquake in November, 1915 and was virtually deserted the following year. [GS]

165. KIMBERLY. Located in White Pine County, 9 miles W of Ely. Date of this card is *circa* 1928. The town was named for Peter L. Kimberly, who was a financier of the Giroux Copper Company, the company that began development of the district in 1903. Kimberly was the southern terminus of the Nevada Northern Railroad, which arrived there in 1906. By 1914 Nevada Consolidated Copper Company had bought out the Giroux interests. The camp, which was a company town, had housing for several hundred workers, a school, hospital, railroad depot, telephone exchange, and Wells Fargo Agency. [NHS]

166. LAHONTAN. Located in Churchill County, 16 miles W of Fallon. As a part of the Truckee Carson Irrigation Project, work on the Lahontan Dam was begun in 1911 and completed in 1915. A hydro-electric plant furnished power to Fallon and nearby communities. Lahontan post office was established November 15, 1911 and discontinued May 31, 1916. Message on card reads: "Came to Nevada in March [1914] . Will probably winter here. There are 300 men working here and about 60 families. This is the Lahontan storage dam. It is on the Carson River about 40 miles east of Carson [City] ." Card is dated July 6, 1914. [GS]

167. LAMOILLE. Located in Elko County, 20 miles SE of Elko. A view of the Lamoille Hotel & Mercantile Company, *circa* 1911, which offered guests comfortable rooms, a barber shop, dining room and bar. The hotel was owned by George F. Talbot, who was District Attorney (1884-1886) of Elko County. In 1890 he was elected Judge of the Fourth Judicial District of Nevada. In 1902 he was elected to the Supreme Court of Nevada and later became its Chief Justice. For several years he was President of the Nevada Historical Society. [RONL]

168. LAMOILLE. The Lamoille Creamery was owned in 1907 by J. F. Holland, a stock breeder in the Lamoille Valley. At that time it was one of the most modern operations of its kind and produced $21,000 worth of butter in a year. Situated in a fertile valley with an abundant water supply, the area was a center of stock breeding, ranching, and farming. Lamoille is the gateway to the Ruby Mountains. [RONL]

169. LANE CITY. Located in White Pine County, 4 miles NW of Ely. Lane City was built on the site of Mineral City (1870-1876), and was named for Charles B. Lane, who bought the Chainman Mine here in 1896. Convinced the mine would yield a great fortune, he spent much of his own in an effort to develop the mine and the town. The Nevada Northern Railroad laid track to Lane City and built a station. Date of this card is *circa* 1905 when the town had a local miners' union, school, hotel, stores, and saloons. But when the Chainman Mine failed for lack of paying ore, optimism faded quickly. By 1911, when the post office closed, only a handful of people remained. [PE]

170. LAS VEGAS. County seat of Clark County. A street scene taken at the corner of First and Fremont streets, looking west, *circa* 1911. A portion of the railroad depot may be seen at the end of the street. A townsite was platted in 1905 and lots sold in an auction sponsored by the San Pedro, Los Angeles and Salt Lake Railroad. In those early years, Las Vegas was a railroad town. In 1906 the Las Vegas & Tonopah Railroad was completed, and trains left daily for Rhyolite, Beatty, Goldfield, and Tonopah. Along Fremont Street there were hotels, restaurants, and stores. The colonnades at extreme right are part of the First State Bank Building. [NSMHS]

171. LAS VEGAS. The Arizona Club was originally a small wooden building on North First Street between Ogden and Stewart streets. In 1906 it moved into a new building of decorated concrete blocks, exterior colonnades, iron grillwork, and entrance windows of leaded glass. Inside, an expansive and elaborate mahogany bar ran the length of the room, with a mirrored back-bar. The ceiling was of embossed tin tiles from which hung fancy electric light fixtures. In 1907 the club was acquired by Al James, who advertised it as the finest saloon in Southern Nevada. [PE]

172. LAS VEGAS. Completed in 1905, the Mission Revival style depot was built by the San Pedro, Los Angeles and Salt Lake Railroad, and acquired by the Union Pacific in 1921. On the second floor was the dispatcher's office. On the ground floor was the waiting room, express and telegraph offices, and baggage rooms. This depot also served the Las Vegas & Tonopah Railroad, which began running trains into the Bullfrog District later in 1906. The depot stood at the head of Fremont Street. It was razed in 1940. [PE]

173. LAS VEGAS. The First State Bank of Las Vegas was organized in March, 1905. At the time this card was made, *circa* 1918, J. Ross Clark was president; W. R. Bracken, vice-president; John S. Park, cashier. The bank remained solvent during the financial panic of 1907, one of the few in Nevada to do so, and played an important part in the early development of Las Vegas. It was located at First and Fremont streets. In later years the bank was purchased by First National Bank of Nevada, which in turn later became First Interstate Bank, and today Wells Fargo Bank. The building was demolished in 1957. [RG]

174. LAS VEGAS. This card shows the town center as it appeared *circa* 1916. On the left is the Majestic Theater, owned by C. P. Squires, which opened for business April 16, 1912, in the old Griffith Block, which also housed the post office. A poster on the sidewalk in front of the Majestic advertises the silent movie, "The Lady Who Lied," which was released in 1915. At the end of the street is the railroad depot, completed in 1905. With the coming of the railroad, the population increased from 1,000 in 1908 to 1,750 in 1915. [RG]

175. LAS VEGAS. The Clark County courthouse was dedicated December 7, 1914. Prior to 1909, Las Vegas was in Lincoln County, and Pioche was the county seat. Geographically, Lincoln County was the second largest in the nation, almost 20,000 square miles. With the growth of Las Vegas, Caliente, and Searchlight, a movement grew for county division, to create a new county for the southern portion. In February, 1909 Governor Dickerson signed a bill creating Clark County, and in a special election Las Vegas was chosen the county seat. [RG]

176. LAS VEGAS. Originally a farm of 80 acres, David G. Lorenzi developed a private resort on this property in 1922, creating the artificial lake shown here, club house, swimming pool, band shell, and picnic grove. For many years it was a popular recreation area, an "oasis in the desert." When gambling was legalized in 1931, the Monte Carlo Casino opened in the park. In 1943 Lorenzi retired and sold his resort to Lloyd St. John, who continued to operate it until 1965, when it was sold to the city and became a municipal park. [NSMHS]

177. LAS VEGAS. Built in 1911, and with such modern facilities as a central heating plant and electric ceiling fans, the Las Vegas School was a combination grade and high school, located at Fourth and Bridger streets. When Las Vegas High School was built in 1929 at the corner of Second and Bridger streets, it became known as the Fifth Street Grammar School. Grade school teachers were paid a salary of $95 a month. Louis J. Oakes was principal of the school from 1921 until 1923, when he went into the photography business and opened the "Vegas Studio." This photograph by Oakes is *circa* 1922. Before the days of air-conditioning, summer vacations began in mid-May, and Easter and Christmas vacations were shortened to make up the time. The building was razed in the 1960's to make way for the Foley Federal Building. [RG]

178. LAS VEGAS. Regular air-mail service was inaugurated on April 17, 1926, and on this occasion photographer Leon Oakes was on hand to record the meeting of the new and the old. The horseman is Bill Morgan and the pilot is Fred Kelly, who later became president of Western Airlines. The other three pilots who flew the run between Los Angeles and Salt Lake City were Jimmie James, Al DeGarmo, and Maury Graham, who navigated the route by following the railroad tracks between Los Angeles, Las Vegas, and Salt Lake City. [NSMHS]

179. LAWTON HOT SPRINGS. Located in Washoe County, 5 miles W of Reno. This place was known as Granite Hot Springs in 1884-85, later named Lawton Hot Springs after its owner, Samuel Lawton. In 1906 it was proposed by the Reno Traction Company to build an electric line to Lawton Hot Springs, but the project was abandoned due to lack of support. [PE]

180. LEHMAN CAVES. Discovered in 1878 by Abe Lehman, when a wagon he was driving broke through the earth's crust and revealed the caverns below. The caverns extend 1,400 feet from the entrance to a depth of 200 feet. Prior to their discovery, there had been no natural entrance. For several years Lehman explored the caves and charged admission to visitors. In 1922 the place was designated a National Monument. Opening Day was August 6, 1922 when a crowd of some 500 people attended, as shown in this photograph. Today the caves are part of Great Basin National Park, administered by the National Park Service. [ROGL]

181. LIDA. Located in Esmeralda County, 27 miles SW of Goldfield. A panorama photo view, postmarked Lida and dated 1905. The town was first settled in the 1870's when gold deposits were worked here. Lacking adequate mills (and significant quantities of ore), the ore had to be freighted to distant Belmont, which proved an inefficient and expensive process. Mining was intermittent until the end of the century, and by 1897 the town was almost deserted. But with the Tonopah-Goldfield boom, Lida revived briefly. There were several stores, a newspaper, bank, saloons, and rooming houses. But the boom was brief. The bank failed, the newspaper folded, and the population drifted on to the next boomtown. [PE]

182. LIDA. Some local wag with a sense of humor wrote a caption for this card: "Mayor of Lida and Family." Probably there was no mayor in Lida, which was an unincorporated town, and the barb may reflect a cynical attitude toward the town's prospects. [PE]

183. LORENA. Located in Mineral County, 1 mile from Bovard. Like its sister camp of Bovard, Lorena was a spin-off of the Rawhide excitement. Here a group poses on Main Street for their photograph in 1908. The tents are makeshift and ephemeral, but the expressions on the faces of these people are not. They look an adventurous and determined lot. Lorena had no ore, only hopes. It had no water either, save what was brought in on freight wagons daily. When the freighters stopped deliveries of water, the camp ceased to exist. The people moved over to Bovard, or back to Rawhide. Lorena lasted only during the summer of 1908. [NHS]

184. LOVELOCK. County seat of Pershing County. This card is dated 1910. Signs visible are: "McPherson Bros. Livery Stable," "Harness Saddlery," owned by Frank E. Baker, "Occidental Hotel," owned by Henry W. Fuss, "Lovelock Co. General Merchandise." In the early days Lovelock was the center of a large mining, agricultural, and cattle raising district. Population in 1910 was 900. A U. S. Government Indian School on a 20-acre parcel had been established earlier for members of the Paiute tribe. The town was originally named Lovelock's, after George Lovelock, a settler from England, but was changed to Lovelock in the census of 1910. [RG]

185. LOVELOCK. Date of this card is *circa* 1913. A passenger train of the Southern Pacific prepares to take on passengers, as trainmen handle baggage. For those passengers who got off at Lovelock bound for the mining camps, there were auto stages that made daily trips to Seven Troughs, Vernon, Farrell, and Rochester. [RONL]

186. LOVELOCK. The stagecoach was still in use in Nevada as late as 1907. Here a coach is about to leave for the Seven Troughs Mining District. Note the dog between the driver and the man sitting on the box. Automobiles were slowly replacing the stagecoach as a means of transportation, even though an auto might be considerably more expensive than a team of horses. Auto stages with hired drivers would meet passengers at the nearest railroad station and drive them to remote mining camps, competing with the stagecoach. The period 1907-10 was one of transition; after 1910 there were few stagecoaches making scheduled runs. [JG]

187. LOVELOCK. Card is postmarked 1910 and shows a portion of the residential area with the business district in the distance behind the windmill. During the years 1907-15, Lovelock gained new importance with the discovery of gold in the Seven Troughs Mining District and the Rochester Mining District. Supplies and machinery came in on the railroad to Lovelock, where they were unloaded and transported to the new mining camps. [RG]

188. LUCKY BOY. Located in Mineral County, 5 miles SW of Hawthorne. This card is one of several made by N. E. Johnson at the time of the Lucky Boy excitement (1909-12), and shows ore being loaded on wagons for shipment. Many of the mines at Lucky Boy were worked by lease arrangements, as they had been in the early days at Goldfield. The district and town were named Lucky Boy by two stage drivers who stopped on the grade to repair an axle and found nearby an outcropping of lead and silver. The mines yielded $1 million to leasers, but by 1914 were nearly worked out, and only 40 people remained. [PE]

189. LUCKY BOY. Silver and lead deposits were first discovered here in 1906 but were not developed in a large way until 1909, when a rush developed and a townsite was laid out. At the peak of the boom the camp had a population of several hundred people, stores, assay office, saloons, and regular stage service to Hawthorne. Lucky Boy was built on a high ridge in the Wassuk Range, on the road from Hawthorne to Aurora and Bodie, California. Date of this card is *circa* 1909. [NHS]

190. LUCKY BOY. Lucky Boy and Hawthorne were neighboring towns, some five miles apart, so the baseball team represented both communities, which gave it an unusual distinction. Here the team poses for a photograph in and beside an automobile—boy with bats is the batboy, and the spotted burro must be the team mascot. Date of card is *circa* 1910. [ROGL]

191. LUDWIG. Located in Lyon County, 5 miles W of Yerington. The copper camp of Ludwig prospered after 1911, when it became the southern terminus of the Nevada Copper Belt Railroad. Mills were built, money invested, and the camp had a population of 750 people, with a school, hotel, telephone service, store, and small hospital. Copper production was $4.25 million through 1926, supplemented by substantial gypsum production for several years. By 1933 the mines had closed and the Nevada Copper Belt discontinued trains to Ludwig in July of that year. [GS]

192. LUDWIG. An early view of the gypsum quarry at Ludwig, which used horses and mules for excavation and transport. A cluster of tents can be seen at center right, used for housing workers. Later in the 1920's, the quarry was worked with mechanized equipment. Among its many uses, gypsum is used as a soil conditioner and for making plaster. [ROGL]

193. LUNING. Located in Mineral County, 25 miles E of Hawthorne. This card is postmarked Luning, dated October 30, 1910. Message reads: "This is a view from my cabin during a recent storm. The heavy clouds shut off the mountains. W. E. P." The writer was probably a prospector working in the Gabbs Range in the Garfield Mining District, who took this photograph and mailed the negative to a film developer to have a few post cards made to send to relatives and friends. With the photographic post card, it was possible to send a personal on-the-spot picture across the country through the mail—in this case a photograph of a lonely cabin high in the remote vastness of Mineral County, mailed to a lady friend in Buffalo, New York. [GS]

194. MANHATTAN. Located in Nye County, 50 miles NNE of Tonopah. As early as 1866 there was a small settlement here. But it was not until 1905 when high grade ore was found that Manhattan came into prominence. Almost overnight a town appeared: banks, hotels, newspapers, stores, saloons, and some 3,000 people eager for a share of the riches. Much of the boom was financed with money from San Francisco investors, but after the earthquake struck there in 1906 money was scarce, and Manhattan slumped. However, new discoveries were made in 1912 and the town revived. [RONL]

195. MANHATTAN. In 1908 Manhattan had a population of 2,000, a stock exchange, two hospitals, electric light plant, water system, schools, and was considered one of the most promising mining towns in Nevada. Exploration and new discoveries continued, and as new mills were built, production increased. In 1912 the Big Four Mining Group consolidated a number of small mines and drew new investment capital into the district. Caption on card reads: "Flood on Main Street, Manhattan, Nev., 1916." [RG]

196. MANHATTAN. The Richards Building is listed in Polk's, *Nevada State Gazetteer*, 1907-08, in the Manhattan listings, Charles L. Richards, lawyer, Richards Building, Main Street. The Manhattan Hotel is listed in the 1914-15 *Gazetteer*, Joseph Plourd, proprietor. This photo card is *circa* 1914. [RG]

197. MANHATTAN. The Manhattan baseball team, *circa* 1912. Note the letter "M" within a diamond design on the jerseys, and a portion of "Manhattan" on the jersey of the young man in the white uniform, kneeling in front row. The two men standing (not in uniform) are probably the coach and manager of the team. The young man kneeling in front (not in uniform) may be the team mascot, or someone who insisted on appearing in the photograph. [RG]

198. MARY MINE. Located in Esmeralda County, 5 miles W of Blair, 30 miles NW of Goldfield. The Mary Mine was a small settlement with its own post office from 1909 to 1914. There was also a boarding house, telephone exchange, electric plant, and saloon. Population in 1914 was 150. The Mary Mine was operated in conjunction with the Drinkwater Mine, connected by underground tunnels, and they shared the same aerial tramway for hauling ore out of the mines. There was daily stage service except Sundays to Blair. Today the property is the site of an open-pit gold mine. [NHS]

199. MASON. Located in Lyon County, 3 miles SW of Yerington. This card is dated 1910, one year after the townsite was surveyed and laid out. The town grew rapidly with the discovery of copper deposits, even moreso when the Nevada Copper Belt Railroad was built through the district in 1910. The railroad built its roundhouse, yards, shops and general offices in Mason. Population at this time was 500. A large copper smelter was built at nearby Thompson. Mason had a water and telephone system, electric power, stores, bank, hotel, and by 1914, a hospital. The surrounding area, watered by the Walker River, was a fertile agricultural area with 100,000 acres under cultivation. [RONL]

200 .MASON. The pond in the foreground was fed by water from the Walker River. This view shows the two-story Mason Hotel in the distance, the school, and several wood-frame commercial buildings, *circa* 1912. Mason reached the peak of its production during World War I when the demand for copper was great, and again in the 1960's when the Weeds Heights Mine was put into production. When the copper boom faded, ranching and agriculture along the Walker River became the economic mainstay of the district. [PE]

201. MASON. This card, postmarked 1911, shows the Mason Hotel, which had opened for business early that same year. The Mason Townsite Company (note the lettering on the awning) had its offices in the building and promoted the town with advertisements that read: "Mines to the west, agriculture to the east, North, and South, smelter to the North. Great opportunities." [RL]

202. MASON. The Nevada Copper Belt Railroad commenced operations January 14, 1910 with a passenger run from Wabuska to Yerington. The line was later extended to Mason and Nordyke, then to Wilson Canyon and Ludwig. The railroad was heavily dependent upon the copper mines for its revenue, and when copper mining declined in the district the railroad cut its operations. Finally, on August 21, 1946, operations ceased altogether. [PE]

203. MAZUMA. Located in Pershing County, in the Seven Troughs Mining District, 25 miles NW of Lovelock. This photograph by Lee Jellums shows Mazuma in its early stages of development, *circa* 1907. The large building at upper left is the Nevada-Darby Mill. At this time the camp had a bank, several stores, hotel, newspaper, post office, baseball team, and school. The three-story building at top right center is the Hotel Mazuma. The Mazuma Hills Mine was the leading producer in the area, located above the town in Seven Troughs Canyon. The townsite was laid out at the mouth of Seven Troughs Canyon, a choice no one questioned at the time, but which later proved most unwise. This card shows Mazuma as it appeared before disaster struck. [RG]

204. MAZUMA. The interesting thing about this photograph is not the roulette game at the Blue Hen Saloon or the players who will probably lose on the next spin of the wheel, but the sign on the wall to the right of the croupier's hat. H. Lee Jellum was the photographer who made many photo cards of the Seven Troughs Mining District. The sign is an advertisement for his post cards, which were probably for sale in the Blue Hen. Many of his cards bear his logo: "Lee Jellum, Photo." —or some variation thereof. [PE]

205.   MAZUMA. One of the most destructive flash floods in Nevada history struck Mazuma on July 19, 1912, when a cloudburst struck over Seven Troughs Canyon and destroyed the town. A wall of water twenty feet high swept everything in its path. Eight people were killed and many injured. The Mazuma Hotel was demolished. The lower two floors were left a pile of debris. The third floor had been ripped off by the crest of the wave and swept down the canyon a mile away. So great was the power of the flood that it swept everything in its path—automobiles, buildings, even the large steel bank vault— and deposited them on the plain below the canyon. One body was discovered the next day seven miles from the town-site. [RONL]

206. MAZUMA. Another view of the flood's aftermath, showing one building demolished, others swept off their foundations. This card is dated July 27, 1912 and message reads: "Was called here to help care for the victims of that dreadful flood caused by that cloud burst you must have read of. This picture was taken a few days ago . . . It's where the town was and you can see the mill I marked with an X caught fire yesterday and burnt down. It stood just across the ravine where we have all the victims who survived. Oh but I shall be glad to get away from here and back to good old Reno." [RG]

207. McDERMITT. Located in Humboldt County, 82 miles N of Winnemucca. The main attraction in McDermitt on July 4, 1914 was undoubtedly the boxing match, photographed by R. W. Heck, of Burns, Oregon. The contestants were Sing Hosan, a Korean from Boise, Idaho, v.s. Hank O'Connell, from Jordan Valley, Oregon. O'Connell won the match in the fifth round on a foul. Boxing was a popular spectator sport in early Nevada with world class matches, such as the Fitzsimmons-Corbett fight in Carson City, the Gans-Nelson fight in Goldfield, the Johnson-Jeffries fight in Reno, and others. While the match at McDermitt was certainly not in that class, it was of sufficient interest in that sparsely-populated region to draw a respectable crowd. [GS]

208. McDERMITT. Established as a trading center for Fort McDermitt and the surrounding stock-raising area, the town straddles the state line between Oregon and Nevada, partly in Malheur County, Oregon, partly in Humboldt County, Nevada. In this photo taken July 4, 1914, the Ora-Vada Hotel is decorated with flags and bunting, as are many of the automobiles. To the left in the stone building is the local black-smith shop. Behind it is the Barn Saloon, appropriately housed in a barn. This photograph was also made by R. W. Heck of Burns, Oregon. [GS]

209. McGILL. Located in White Pine County, 9 miles N of Ely. McGill was known as Smelter from September 7, 1907 until August 14, 1908 when the name was changed back to McGill. Photo shows the works of the Steptoe Valley Smelting & Mining Company. In April, 1912 concentrate output from the mines reached 14,168 tons and required 253 cars of the Nevada Northern Railroad to move it to McGill. At that rate of production the dollar value of the ore was second highest in Nevada, exceeded only by the glory days of the Comstock. In 1913 the McGill plant was jointly owned by the Guggenheim interests and Nevada Consolidated Copper. [RONL]

210. McGILL. A view of the concentrator plant at McGill, 1908. Inside the tiered plant was a grinding section where huge ball mills reduced ore to powder, and then through a flotation process to extract the metals. The smelter was located a short distance from the concentrator plant. At the upper right a portion of the long trestle can be seen which was 1,700 feet in length, along which ore cars brought ore to the plant. In 1922 the entire plant and trestle were destroyed by fire. A new and more efficient plant was quickly built to replace it. [RONL]

211. McGILL. The first football game in White Pine County was played in November, 1909 between McGill and Ely, the only towns in the district to field football teams. Uniforms and other expenses were paid for by the copper companies. Rivalry between the two teams was keen, and the annual Thanksgiving Day game was the highlight of the season. [ROGL]

212. METROPOLIS. Located in Elko County, 12 miles NW of Wells. Metropolis was created by the Pacific Reclamation Company as the centerpiece of an agricultural empire. The company owned 40,000 acres of land along Bishop Creek, built a large storage dam to store water for irrigation, and sold acreage to hopeful farmers. But in 1912 a court action was filed contesting the company's water rights. The company lost the suit, with rights to irrigate only 4,000 acres instead of 40,000. The company turned to dry-farming methods, and helped by a wet year in 1914, produced some impressive crops, including the Turkey Red Wheat shown in this view. But several dry years followed, the company lost its appeal in court, and by 1917 the disillusioned farmers began to leave. [NNM]

213. METROPOLIS. A more expansive view of the townsite, but not showing the Metropolis Hotel, one of the landmarks of the town. The building to the left of the depot is the Western Lumber Company yards. The structure at far right is part of the Consolidated Wagon Works. A townsite was surveyed with broad avenues, parks, and sidewalks. A large brick schoolhouse, named the Lincoln School, was built and electric lights installed along the streets. In 1911 over a mile and a half of concrete sidewalks were laid around the town. A water system, bringing water from springs at Trout Creek, was completed in 1912. But Metropolis never became a metropolis. A few years later the town was almost deserted. [NNM]

214. METROPOLIS. The Southern Pacific Railroad depot was opened for business on March 16, 1912, although the railroad had been bringing passengers and freight to Metropolis for several months. Service was over a branch line from Carlin and Wells. The depot at Metropolis was larger than those at Carlin and Wells, reflecting the optimism of town boosters, and was landscaped with flower beds and a gushing fountain. The building had a concrete basement with a steam-heating plant, ticket and telegraph office, waiting room, express office, and living quarters for the station agent on the second floor. [NNM]

215. METROPOLIS. The Metropolis Hotel opened on December 29, 1911 with a lavish banquet and reception for guests as far away as Salt Lake City. The size and opulence of the hotel reflected the hopes of its builders that Metropolis would become the largest city in Nevada. The building was three stories with an exterior of red brick, interiors decorated with costly furnishings and tiled floors, electricity throughout powered by a huge generator in the basement, elevator, private baths, dining room, barber shop, drug store, and bar. The hotel closed for lack of business in 1913 and by 1920 the building was abandoned. Afterward, it was inhabited only by bats and owls. It was destroyed by fire in the early 1930's. This view, made in 1921, shows the hotel in a derelict state. [ROGL]

216. MIDAS. Located in Elko County, 42 miles NE of Golconda. This view is dated 1908 and shows the Main Street, a collection of frame buildings and tents. At the peak of the boom in 1908 the town had a newspaper, general merchandise stores, boarding houses, assay office, and twenty saloons. But by the spring of next year the excitement had waned and many of the gold-camp drifters had moved elsewhere. In 1915 a mill was built, and another in 1926, and several mines were still working in the 1920's. Activity after 1927 was intermittent. Total production for the district was under $1 million. [JG]

217. MIDAS. In 1907 the town had been known as Gold Circle. The name was changed to Midas in 1908. This photograph is an early view of the camp, dated "May 1, 08," one year after discovery of the Elko Prince Mine. Many of the structures shown are tents, but there is a clearly defined street, with tents and buildings in the far distance, the site of a promotional camp known briefly as Summit, two miles south. During the summer of 1908 the town claimed a population of 2,000. Gold and silver were produced from several mines into the 1920's, after which the town went into rapid decline . [RG]

218. MIDAS. Caption on card reads: "Getting Ready for the First Horse Race." Amateur horseracing was a popular form of entertainment in the mining camps. Boxing matches were probably the most popular of all. Jack Dempsey lived briefly in Midas, where he worked as a miner and did his road work by running to and from his claim every day. Dempsey may have had an unpublicized match or two in Midas, but he did not attract attention until he fought Johnny Sudenberg in Goldfield and Tonopah in 1915. [PE]

219. MILLERS. Located in Esmeralda County, 13 miles W of Tonopah. Millers was the site of two large mills for processing ores from Tonopah—the Desert Power & Milling Company and the Tonopah-Belmont Mill—and an important station and rolling stock repair yard for the Tonopah & Goldfield Railroad, which carried large shipments of ore to the mills. The town had a population of 275 in 1914, a business section with saloons and a hotel. The town prospered with employment from the mills and railroad, but declined in later years when ore was shipped elsewhere for milling. The large building at left was the Las Palmas Hotel, owned by Mrs. Dorcus Wigstead. [PE]

220. MILLERS. A view of the 100-stamp mill of the Desert Power & Milling Company, built by the Tonopah Mining Company in 1906. The large mound at right center is one of several slag heaps. The design of the plant was similar to the Butters Plant in Virginia City, which in turn was based upon the latest technology used in South Africa. A high recovery rate was obtained—about 90% for gold and 86% for silver. [PE]

221. MILLETT. Located in Nye County, 65 miles N of Tonopah. This settlement was first known as the Scheel Ranch, a stage station in the Smoky Valley, changed to Millett in the 1890's. In 1906 gold ore was found in nearby Toiyabe Mountains and a small camp formed around the ranch, including a blacksmith shop, boarding house, and saloon. The camp had telephone connections and daily stage service with Austin and Manhattan. The Manuel Mining Company was the largest in the district, owned by J. A. Vincent, F. P. Carey, superintendent. The camp had a population of 100 in 1908. Mining ceased after a couple of years. The store continued to serve as a trading center in the Smoky Valley. [RM]

222. MINA. Located in Mineral County, 34 miles E of Hawthorne. Date of this photo card is *circa* 1909. The town was originally a station on the Carson & Colorado Railroad, later a division point on the Nevada & California Railroad, which built a large roundhouse here in 1905, machine shops, and railroad yards. Signs visible in this view are: Mina Mercantile Company, owned by Solomon M. Summerfield; Davis Hotel, owned by W. Hastings Davis; Miners and Merchants Bank, owned by Frank B. Baker. The building with the large balcony porch was the Mina Hotel, which advertised sixty rooms, a large dining room, and first class bar. [NHS]

223. MINA. Caption on card reads: "S. P. Narrow Gauge, Mina, Nev." Card is dated 1916. Mina was created in 1905 as the southern terminus of the newly-created Nevada & California Railroad, formerly known as the Carson & Colorado, acquired by Southern Pacific in 1905. Southbound trains connected with the Tonopah & Goldfield Railroad at Mina, and during the Tonopah-Goldfield boom years there was heavy traffic over the line, both passengers and freight. In 1907 there were 250 railroad employees in Mina. The Nevada & California also ran trains out of the Mina terminal into California, through the Owens Valley, to Keeler. [PE]

224. MINDEN. Located in Douglas County, 15 miles S of Carson City. A view of the Minden Warehouse Company, owned and operated by John B. and H. F. Dangberg. The Dangberg family also owned the Dangberg Land & Livestock Company, the Minden Flour Milling Company, and the Carson Valley Hay & Produce Company. In 1914 Minden had a population of 150, was the southern terminus of the Virginia & Truckee Railroad, and was the center of a prosperous agricultural and livestock district. [RONL]

225. MINDEN. The Minden Inn was completed in 1916 and was called "the little St. Francis," being the finest hotel in the area. The architect was well-known Frederick J. DeLongchamps, and the building was designed along neo-classical lines. It was financed by the Dangberg family, and included the latest improvements, including steam heat and an elevator. The building has since been remodeled and is leased to Douglas County to house county offices. [NHS]

226. MINDEN. Card is dated October 15, 1911 and was mailed by one of the children in the photograph who wrote: "I will send you one of the photos of the Minden school." Picture shows six girls in front row, six boys in back, teacher at right. The school itself was literally a one-room schoolhouse. Note the bicycle at left. [JG]

227. MINERAL HILL. Located in Eureka County, 32 miles S of Carlin. This double-size photo card shows Mineral Hill in a state of decline, *circa* 1912. The large building at left with the peaked roof is the old Atwood Mill, which appears in disuse. Rich silver float was discovered here in 1869. In 1871 the properties were consolidated by an English consortium into the California Mining Company, but by 1873 the richest deposits had been worked out. It is estimated that the mines produced some $1.5 million in silver through 1874. Afterward, small leasers continued to work the property. The mines were located on the hill in back of the camp; several tailing dumps are visible, and roads leading up to the mines. The 1910 census listed a population of 50. [JJ]

228. MOAPA. Located in Clark County, 51 miles NW of Las Vegas. Originally home to a band of southern Paiute Indians, the valley was colonized by Mormons in 1865. Moapa became a station on the San Pedro, Los Angeles and Salt Lake Railroad in 1905. Date of this card is *circa* 1912, and shows the depot at left center, the Nevada Club Saloon, W. C. Bowman, General Merchandise, and W. C. Bowman, Lumber, Hay & Flour. Bowman is mentioned in the *Las Vegas Age* as an official of the Muddy Valley Irrigation Co., registry agent for the railroad, and owner of the Moapa Commercial Company. In 1912 he was Justice of the Peace here. In 1910 a reservation was established for the southern Paiute, and the census for that year shows a population of 2,027 on the reservation. The tribe raised cattle and alfalfa, with approximately 6,000 acres under cultivation. There were 30 Paiute children attending the reservation school in 1910. [RONL]

229. MOANA SPRINGS. Located in Washoe County, 2 miles S of downtown Reno. A popular spa and resort around 1910 and for many years afterward. It was a favorite spot for family picnics and social gatherings. In 1910 it was the training camp of Jim Jeffries, former heavyweight boxing champion, just prior to his match with Jack Johnson in Reno. There were facilities for hot baths and a large enclosed swimming pool. The large building shown here was razed in the mid-1960's, but there is still an enclosed pool on the site. [RG]

230. MONTELLO. Located in Elko County, 120 miles NE of Elko. This large hotel was located alongside the track of the Southern Pacific Railroad, and was known locally as the Southern Pacific Hotel. Montello was the eastern-most division point on the Southern Pacific and the last stop before crossing the Great Salt Lake. The town was created by the railroad in 1905, when shops, yards, and a roundhouse were built. In 1908 the population was 200. By 1915 it had increased to 800. After 1950 Montello lost its importance as a railroad town when most of the shop facilities, including the roundhouse, were moved to Ogden, Utah. [PE]

231. MOUND HOUSE. Located in Lyon County, 6 miles SW of Dayton. Originally a station on a private toll road, Mound House is best remembered as a railroad junction point. The Virginia & Truckee arrived here in 1869, and the Carson & Colorado in 1881. With the boom at Tonopah and Goldfield in the early part of this century, Mound House was a point of origin for southbound trains. In 1913 the Pacific Portland Cement Company built a gypsum plant (shown here), which for a time provided much needed revenue for the languishing Virginia & Truckee. [GS]

232. MOUNTAIN CITY. Located in Elko County, 85 miles N of Elko. The town had its beginnings in 1868 when gold was discovered by Chinese miners. In 1872 a boom was underway and a considerable town developed. Many buildings were erected, some of brick and stone. Mountain City cast 1,800 votes in the Grant presidential election. By 1875, however, several mines had closed, and the town went into a temporary decline. This is a promotional-type card, issued to promote or boost the town, dated October 1, 1908. [GS]

233. MOUNTAIN CITY. The Nelson Mill was in operation shortly after the turn of the century, when there was a revival in gold mining here. This was followed by yet another decline in the fortunes of Mountain City, and the town was nearly abandoned. But when rich copper deposits were discovered in 1931, still another revival followed with the development of the Rio Tinto Mine. Total production for Mountain City is estimated at about $14 million, including silver, gold, and copper. [GS]

234. NATIONAL. Located in Humboldt County, 74 miles N of Winnemucca. Gold and silver were discovered here in 1907 by J. L. Workman, an automobile-traveling prospector who named the camp after his automobile, a National. At a depth of only forty feet, the incredibly rich National vein was struck, almost pure electrum, which assayed at the unheard figure of $30 thousand a ton. The ore was so rich that armed guards were hired to protect the National Mine. The National Mine continued producing rich ore through 1915, when it finally closed, the ore mined out. But it was a spectacular run while it lasted, producing $7 million, not including what might have been highgraded out of the mine. [NHS]

235. NATIONAL. Comparing this photo card with the one above—especially the printed captions on both—it is logical to assume they were made by the same anonymous photographer. The type style is the same, and the stock numbers—855 and 867—are close together in numerical sequence, suggesting the photographer may have made as many as a dozen different views of National. There is also a card of the Stall Brothers Lease, no. 860 in the series. They were likely made by a traveling photographer on the same day, and placed for consignment . In any case, they are rare cards and probably not more than a few dozen were made for each view. [PE]

236. NATIONAL. Photo shows the town center, National Hotel at right. The first issue of the *National Miner* came out in the summer of 1910, and the population had reached a peak of over 600 people, but not all of them permanent residents. A schoolhouse was built through private subscription and donated labor, and some forty children enrolled the first year. The town had a livery stable, general store, restaurants, saloons, an undertaker, assay office, physician, laundry and bath house. [ROGL]

237. NELSON. Located in Clark County, 29 miles S of Boulder City. Card is postmarked Nelson and dated May 26, 1910. This tent camp was probably near Nelson in the El Dorado Mining District. In 1905 there was a revival in the district and Nelson replaced the old camp of El Dorado as the commercial center. A post office was established June 17, 1905. Several mines were developed, producing gold, silver, copper, and lead. The oldest mine in the district, the Techatticup, located in 1862, was the richest in the district, said to have produced over $5 million during its long life. [RONL]

238. NIXON. Located in Washoe County, 17 miles NNW of Wadsworth. A view of the trading post, *circa* 1928, when the settlement was the center of the Pyramid Lake Paiute Indian Reservation. In 1910 the population of the reservation was 600. It was named for George S. Nixon, U. S. Senator from Nevada, 1905-1911. A post office was established August 22, 1912. [PE]

239. NORDYKE. Located in Lyon County, 8 miles SSW of Yerington. An agricultural settlement on the Walker River, at the edge of the Mason Valley, and the site of a flour mill built in 1891. The mill was owned and operated by J. I. and J. W. Wilson. A quartz mill was built here around 1905, powered by water from the Walker River. In 1909 the population was 35. In 1910 Nordyke became a station on the Nevada Copper Belt Railroad, but the coming of the railroad failed to rescue the settlement from obscurity. A post office served the settlement from June, 1892 until January, 1914. [JG]

240. OLINGHOUSE. Located in Washoe County, 40 miles E of Reno. Olinghouse experienced a mining boom from 1900 until 1907, when news of a series of new strikes were widely reported. This view, made in 1908, shows the Crosby and McCoy Hotel at bottom center, and immediately to the left, the Pioneer Saloon. Another saloon, with the novel name of Gouge Eye, also housed the assay office. In 1907 the Nevada Railroad Company finished laying track from Wadsworth to Olinghouse, and a Railroad Day celebration was held May 28, 1907, with some 800 people on hand, including Governor Sparks. But when ore from the mines declined in values in 1909, the railroad ceased operations. [ROGL]

241. OLINGHOUSE. A closer view of the town, *circa* 1906, before the coming of the railroad. The mining district was first called McClanesburg, later White Horse, and finally Olinghouse. Both these views of Olinghouse are signed "Linton," with no initials or first name. There is, however, a W. D. Linton listed in a 1905 directory as living in Wadsworth, Nevada, engaged in the hotel and mining business. There are several photo post cards of Wadsworth also signed "Linton" and it is possible W. D. Linton of Wadsworth may have been the photographer in question here. [JJ]

242. OREANA STATION. Located in Pershing County, 14 miles NE of Lovelock. This place was originally a station on the Southern Pacific Railroad, so designated in the 1880's. In 1912, with the boom at nearby Rochester, a small town formed around the station, known as the "Gateway to Rochester," including a hotel, saloons, depot, stores, and a post office. Later, when the Nevada Short Line Railroad built a line into Rochester and Nenzel Hill, it chose Oreana Station as the site for its shops and engine house. By 1917 the hectic activity of the boom had subsided as ore shipments declined. The following year Rochester was almost destroyed by a flash flood, and Oreana Station sank into obscurity. Later in the 1920's, it was the site of a general store and gasoline station known as Dad Lee's. [JG]

243. OWYHEE. Located in Elko County, 98 miles N of Elko. The community takes its name from the Owyhee River, which rises in the northern part of Elko County and flows into the Snake River, one of the few rivers in Nevada that eventually flows into the sea instead of a sink. Owyhee is the center of the Duck Valley Indian Reservation (Western Shoshone tribe), established in 1878. The reservation covers 290,000 acres in Nevada and Idaho. In 1913 the Indian population was 569; by the 1930's it had declined to 400. [GS]

244. PALISADE. Located in Eureka County, 10 miles W of Carlin. This card is postmarked Palisade and dated 1909. Shown here is engine no. 7 of the Eureka & Palisade Railroad, with trainmen (one perched atop the bell-frame on the engine). Engine no. 7 was built by the Baldwin Locomotive Works in the early 1880's and was named the P. Evarts, who was superintendent of the line. The Eureka & Palisade was a narrow gauge line that ran from Eureka to Palisade, and over its sixty-five years of operations owned as many as ten locomotives. [PE]

245. PALISADE. The location of the Western Pacific Railroad tunnel paralleled the Southern Pacific line and tunnel just outside Palisade, both lines crossing the tracks of the Eureka & Palisade Railroad and the Humboldt River. By November, 1908 the Western Pacific had laid track from Salt Lake City to Halleck, Nevada, and by Christmas Day, to Elko. [ROGL]

246. PALISADE. The Valley House was owned and operated by A. J. Sasserno in 1907. The hotel catered to the railroad trade as three separate railroads had operations at Palisade. In 1908 the population was 75. [PE]

247. PARADISE VALLEY. Located in Humboldt County, 40 miles NE of Winnemucca. In 1906 the town had a population of 250, had telephone connections with Winnemucca and Golconda, daily stage service, a Methodist and Catholic Church, physician, and several stores. The large building at left center with the pointed cupola is the Auditorium Hotel, a local landmark, which survived into the 1930's, when it was destroyed by fire. It was owned and operated by Alfonso Pasquale. [ROGL]

248. PARADISE VALLEY. Settled in the 1860's, the valley attracted settlers because of its fertile soil and abundant water supply. Although the growing season was short, local orchards produced apples, cherries, pears, peaches, plums, and apricots. A variety of rich grain crops were grown, and a flour mill was built in 1868, which supplied milled flour and cereals for towns throughout Nevada. Wyatt and Virgil Earp lived here briefly in the 1890's. This photograph, *circa* 1908, shows a group of locals in front of the J. B. Case store. Mr. Case also served the community as postmaster and notary public. [RG]

249. PARRAN. Located in Churchill County, 20 miles NE of Hazen. A station and telegraph point on the Southern Pacific Railroad, near the Humboldt Sink. A post office was opened here January 29, 1910 and discontinued July 31, 1913. The 1910 census lists a population of 10. [PE]

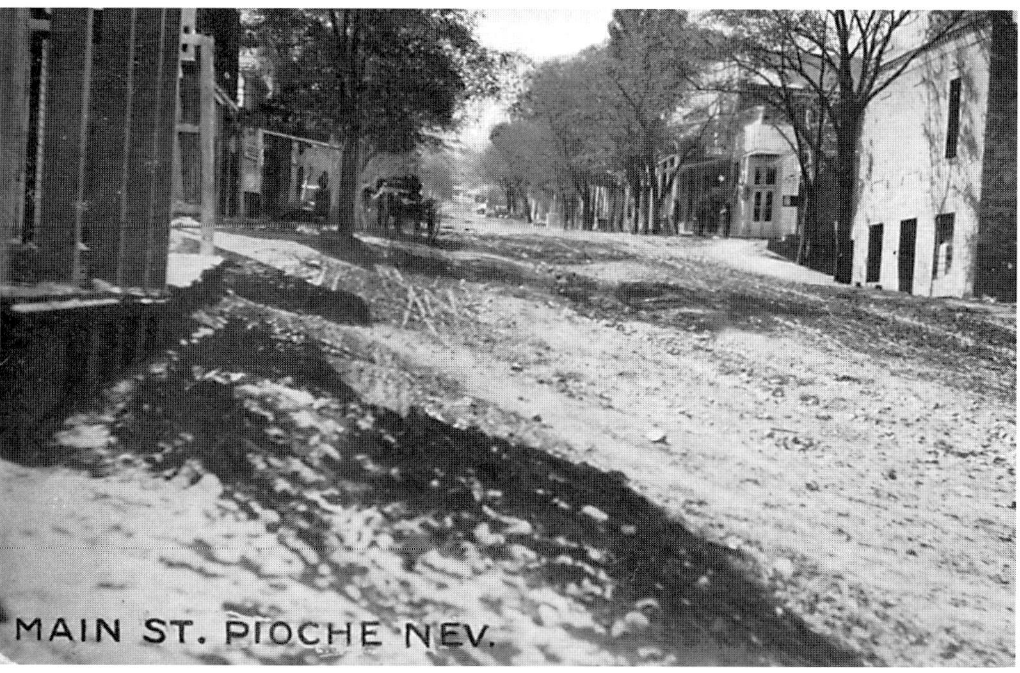

250. PIOCHE. County seat of Lincoln County. Silver discoveries were made as early as 1863 but a mining camp did not take shape until 1868. In the years that followed, up until 1878, Pioche was one of the richest and largest camps in Nevada, and one of the most lawless. Because of its remote location in southeastern Nevada (some 400 miles from the population centers), the town was wide open for many years. Gunslingers walked the streets, murders were commonplace, and mine owners hired professional gunmen for protection. In 1873 the Pioche and Bullionville Railroad came to Pioche, and civilization—albeit slowly—came also. This card was mailed from Pioche in 1912 by a law clerk who had accompanied Judge Taber there for a term of court. [RG]

251. PIOCHE. A view showing the central part of Pioche, 1907. At this time there were still more mining companies listed in the Pioche directory than for any other type of business. The town had a hospital, school, mercantile stores, bank, newspaper, fraternal lodges, telephone and water system, hotels, restaurants, the Pioche Brass Band, Chinese laundry, and even a watchmaker. [RG]

252. PIOCHE. By 1910, when this card was issued, mine production had slackened somewhat, but there was still considerable activity in exploration and in working tailings left over from the old mines and mills. Population at this time was 1,000. During the 1930's mine production increased again with the discovery of lead and zinc deposits. The leading producer of lead and zinc during the period 1937-1957 was Combined Metals Corporation, which built a large mill at Caselton. Total production for that period is estimated at $64 million. [JG]

253. PIOCHE. The Bank of Pioche was incorporated May 11, 1907 and opened for business June 6, 1907, with a capitalization of $25,000. J. F. Tolton was president; G. C. Whitmore, vice-president; and M. C. Fitzpatrick, chief cashier. Ten directors served on the board. [NSMHS]

254. PIONEER. Located in Nye County, 14 miles NW of Beatty. This photo card is dated February 4, 1909 and shows the town center. The principal mines here were the Pioneer and the Mayflower. The town had a newspaper, stage and express office, saloons, restaurants, and assay office. The Montgomery Hotel in Beatty was moved to Pioneer, but it was destroyed in the fire of May, 1909. A post office opened on March 2, 1909, and was discontinued February 19, 1931. [JG]

255. PIONEER. The town was named for the Pioneer Mine, discovered in 1907, and located in the northern part of the Bullfrog District. This photo card is dated March 12, 1909 and shows Pioneer before the fire of May, 1909, which destroyed much of the town. A combination of wooden buildings and tents, the town had a population of 900 in 1909, and was considered one of the most promising camps in the Bullfrog District. The town was partially rebuilt after the 1909 fire, but when projected plans to build a railroad into Pioneer failed for lack of financing (and lack of ore), the population declined to 200 by 1914. The Pioneer Mine was closed in 1916, but occasional leasers continued to operate into the early 1920's. [RG]

256. PROSPECT. Located in Eureka County, 5 miles S of Eureka. A group posed in their Sunday best for this photograph, postmarked Prospect, dated 1907. The building in the background is most probably part of the property of the Diamond Excelsior Mining Company, which was in operation here in 1907. At that time Prospect had a population of 70, with tri-weekly stage service to Eureka. By 1915 the population had dwindled down to 40. The post office was closed in 1918. Mining had begun here in 1882, when dozens of silver claims dotted the area around Prospect Mountain. [JG]

257. QUARTETTE. Located in Clark County, 50 miles S of Las Vegas. "Quartette Mill and Cyanide Plant," *circa* 1909. The Quartette Mine, one of the most productive in the Searchlight District, produced from $200,000 to $400,000 each year from 1903-1909. It continued to operate under leasing agreements until 1921, producing gold, silver, copper and lead. The buildings shown in the distance beyond the mill provided housing for employees. A post office was established here September 15, 1900 and discontinued September 15, 1902. [JG]

258. RAMSEY. Located in Lyon County, 28 miles N of Dayton. The camp was named for Tom and Bladen Ramsey, who staked some 150 claims in the district in 1906. Earlier, the Ramsey brothers had been among the first prospectors on the scene in Goldfield, and had staked Mohawk 1 and 2, which later proved to be the richest ground in Goldfield. They sold prematurely, getting only $10,000 for their two claims. The camp of Ramsey, however, was no Goldfield. It boomed briefly—for three years—and at its peak had a population of 500, with a newspaper, hotels, assay office, stores, saloons, and a post office. [PE]

259. RAWHIDE. Located in Mineral County, 29 miles NE of Schurz. The great Rawhide boom began in the closing weeks of 1907. This photo card, dated "Jan. lst-08," shows a modest collection of tents and wooden buildings, some under construction, on Main Street. The discoveries of the Grutt brothers of seam gold said to assay out at $300,000 a ton attracted wide publicity, and three months later some 5,000 people had rushed into Rawhide. The assay reports were grossly exaggerated, however, more promotional than real. Newspapers in Goldfield and Tonopah publicized the discoveries, copied by the eastern press. Everyone who had missed the boom at Tonopah and Goldfield saw this as a second chance to get in on the ground floor of a new bonanza. [RG]

260. RAWHIDE. Postmarked April 12, 1908 this photo card shows the tremendous growth of Rawhide (when compared to the preceding card) in less than three months. Taken from approximately the same point, one can see Main Street has been extended considerably, and the area beyond has been built up thickly with wooden buildings and tents. At the peak of the boom, Rawhide had three banks (open until midnight), six theaters, hotels, stock exchange, telephone and telegraph service, a red-light district called Stingaree Gulch that rivaled San Francisco's Barbary Coast—and even a refrigeration plant. Everyone firmly believed Rawhide would become the new Goldfield. The roadbed for the Rawhide & Western Railroad had been surveyed, grading was underway, but when Rawhide burned plans for the railroad were abandoned. [RG]

261. RAWHIDE. Caption on front of card reads: "Trying to get there [sic] mail at Rawhide, Nev." The correspondent has marked an "X" for "our office" and the sign reads: "Toggery—tents and bedding." Card is postmarked March 16, 1908 and the message reads: "Giving you an idea of what we are up against on the mail question here." The post office was opened October 11, 1907 and closed August 31, 1941. [RG]

262. RAWHIDE. A roulette game in a Rawhide saloon, presided over by a burly man wearing a derby hat, *circa* 1908. The game appears to be using chips, but was more often played with silver dollars and gold coins. Roulette was the favorite game of the novice, an eastern tenderfoot newly arrived in camp, wanting to participate in the illusion of getting rich quick. The more experienced gambler, usually with an inscrutable face, preferred to play faro or poker. Slot machines, which had recently made their appearance, attracted very little interest. [PE]

263.   RAWHIDE. The disastrous fire in Rawhide on September 4, 1908, made headlines all over the nation. Four volunteer fire companies fought the blaze and over 3,000 pounds of dynamite was used to raze buildings in the path of the fire, to little avail. When the fire had burned itself out, not one building remained in a nine-block area of the business district. Parts of the residential area were also burned. The loss was estimated at $1 million, and 3,000 people had been left homeless. Reno, San Francisco, Tonopah and Goldfield responded immediately by sending over $12 thousand in aid. Today an open-pit gold mine covers much of the old townsite. [ROGL]

264. RED BUTTE. Located in Humboldt County, 15 miles N of Sulphur. This card is dated June 17, 1910 and message reads: "Dear Mother. This is wife, baby, and mother-in-law. 'ha-ha.' Your boy." Perhaps with a pun intended, mother-in-law is in the driver's seat, son-in-law in the back seat. In 1910 the ungraded road to Red Butte was over a difficult terrain, but mother-in-law seems a determined sort and equal to the challenge. Red Butte was a small camp of less than 100 people, the site of a gold and copper strike in 1907. [PE]

265. RENO. County seat of Washoe County. A fine action photograph by William Cann, photographer, of Reno, of a fire on Commercial Row, March 1, 1909 that destroyed the Palace Casino and the Arcade Hotel. The Washoe Saloon was partially damaged but escaped destruction. A huge crowd came to watch the fire, some standing on top of railroad boxcars and the roofs of nearby buildings. Note the ladder and two firemen on the roof of the Washoe Saloon. Message on card reads: "Some of Reno watching the fire. The two buildings were completely destroyed. They were the largest gambling houses in the city and $100,000 went up in smoke." [RG]

266. RENO. "Commercial Row, Reno, Nev." Date of photo is *circa* 1908. Commercial Row, which faced the Southern Pacific Railroad tracks and depot, ran parallel to the railroad property for two blocks. Most of Reno's casinos were located here, as well as several hotels. At far left is the Palace Casino, which was destroyed by fire March 1, 1909. [PE]

267. RENO. The Washoe Saloon was located on Commercial Row. Of the men appearing in this photograph, the man at left appears to be wearing a policeman's uniform. Signs advertise Wieland's Beer, Turkish Trophies cigarettes, apples, oranges, peanuts, pine-nuts, cigars, etc. Around the window-counter at right can be seen a display of post cards. On March 1, 1909 the Washoe Saloon narrowly escaped destruction when a fire destroyed the two adjacent buildings, the Palace Casino and Arcade Hotel. [RG]

268. RENO. Members of the Reno Fire Department in 1909. The man with the walrus mustache in front row center is W. W. Webster, fire-chief. Beginning as a volunteer organization in 1868, the department was put on a professional basis in 1875 when full-time firemen were hired and new equipment was purchased. [ROGL]

269. RENO. William E. Cann, shown here with his family in a flag-decorated automobile, was Reno's most prolific maker of real photo post cards. In the background is the Cann Drugstore (note the Kodak sign) which carried a complete line of cameras and photographic supplies, and a large selection of photo post cards. This photo was taken *circa* 1910, probably on a national holiday, possibly the Fourth of July. [ROGL]

270. RENO. Caption on card reads: "Col. Roosevelt at Reno, Nev." Theodore Roosevelt ran for President on the Progressive (Bull Moose) ticket in 1912, after a split in the Republican Party, and appeared in Reno to address his supporters. Here he appears with a group at the University of Nevada campus, photographed by William Cann. In Nevada, the Progressive Party polled 5,700 votes for Roosevelt, coming in second against the Democratic ticket, whose candidate, Woodrow Wilson, won the national election. [PE]

271. RENO. This photograph was taken at the Reno jail shortly after a posse had engaged Shoshone Mike and his band of renegade Indians near Winnemucca in 1911, in what has been described as the last Indian battle in the United States. Shoshone Mike's band had allegedly murdered four sheep ranchers near Eagleville, California, then made their way across the Black Rock Desert north of Winnemucca. When caught by the posse, the Indians fought to the death, and only three children were taken alive. Even the children fought desperately, using clubs and spears. The man at left is Charles P. Ferrel, Sheriff of Washoe County, a member of the posse, into whose custody the Indian children, shown here, were placed. [RG]

272. RENO. A rare photo of Jack Johnson at his training camp (Rick's Resort) outside of Reno, prior to the Johnson-Jeffries boxing championship match on July 4, 1910. The photographer was William Cann, of Reno. At this time, Johnson held the world title, having won it from Tommy Burns in Sydney, Australia, December 26, 1908. The caption on the card is wrong: Johnson was not married at this time. The woman seated in front of Johnson is Belle Schreiber, who would later betray him and testify against him as the government's star witness when he was indicted under the Mann Act. The men seated on either side of Johnson are members of his training camp crew. [RG]

273. RENO. One of a series of some 120 real photo post cards issued as a set by P. F. Dana, San Francisco photographer, whose studio was at 1354 Fillmore Street. Jeffries had retired undefeated in 1904 to his alfalfa farm in southern California. He had not fought in six years. He was elected by the press and the public as the "White Hope," the only man who might beat Jack Johnson. In the days before the fight Jeffries was the overwhelming favorite. Everyone said he would win—John L. Sullivan, Tommy Burns, Jim Corbett, Jack London, among others. But Jeffries was older and past his prime. Johnson was at the peak of his powers. In the fifteenth round, Jeffries was knocked down, barely rose before the count was over, and his seconds threw in the sponge. It was a match that made boxing history. [RG]

274. RHYOLITE. Located in Nye County, 5 miles W of Beatty. Card is captioned: "Autos galore at Rhyolite," issued by A. E. Holt, of Rhyolite. The town was called the "Queen City of the Desert," and by 1907 the population was 6,000, complete with electric power, telephone service, water companies, a Board of Trade, three railroads, opera house, stock exchange, ice plants, newspapers, and pleasant homes. But the town was built on an optimism the mines could not equal. Every one thought it would become another Goldfield. When the financial panic of 1907 hit the nation, Rhyolite went into decline. By 1910 only 700 people remained. By 1918 it was a ghost. The Bullfrog District produced more than $3 million in gold through 1940, and is active again today. [RG]

275. RHYOLITE. The John S. Cook & Company Bank, fronting on Golden Street, was the most imposing building in Rhyolite. Associated with the Cook Bank in Goldfield, the Rhyolite Bank had its own charter, and therefore was entitled to issue its own national bank notes, and did. Oddly, none are known, and it would seem none have survived. The upper floors of the building housed professional offices. Construction of the building cost $90,000, a considerable sum at the time. A portion of the building still stands, and is one of the most photographed of all ghost town ruins. [RG]

276. RHYOLITE. A rare photo card by A. E. Holt, of Rhyolite, showing Mr. and Mrs. Walter Scott. Scotty met his future bride, Ella Josephine Milius, in 1900 in New York City, while he was a performer with the Buffalo Bill Wild West Show. They were married in Cincinnati, headed west to Cripple Creek, Colorado, where Scotty worked briefly in a gold mine. During the early years of the Bullfrog excitement, Mrs. Scott (whom Scotty called "Jack") lived in Los Angeles, while Scotty periodically emerged from his Death Valley wanderings to put in an appearance at Goldfield, Tonopah, and Rhyolite. This card is proof that Mrs. Scott joined him on at least one occasion, perhaps taking the train from Los Angeles to Rhyolite. [NHS]

277. RHYOLITE. Walter Scott (or "Death Valley Scotty") was a popular legend in his own time, as shown in this photograph by A. E. Holt, dated March 22, 1909. It was widely believed that Scotty had a secret gold mine somewhere in Death Valley. Never one to sell himself short, he encouraged such notions. On visits to camps in the Bullfrog District, he tossed silver dollars to boys who followed him through the streets, flashed rolls of twenty-dollar gold pieces, and in the eyes of admiring hopefuls he was success personified. He never had a secret gold mine in Death Valley or anywhere else, but Scotty was never one to scotch a rumor about himself, especially when it might work to his advantage. [NHS]

278. RHYOLITE. A unique photo card published by A. E. Holt, written by him, and postmarked October 19, 1907. Holt has identified himself in the picture by marking an "X" at his feet. In addition to publishing post cards and taking photographs, Holt also sold real estate, mining properties, insurance, and made collections. He was an enthusiastic booster of Rhyolite. This card was mailed from Rhyolite to E. J. Chadwick, of Goldfield, and reads: "How are you making it Chadwick? Here is a picture of my office. Came by your office before I left the other day but you were not in. Better come down here and see Rhyolite. Good luck to you." [RG]

279. RHYOLITE. The Montgomery-Shoshone Mine was discovered in 1904 when a Shoshone Indian by the name of Shoshone Mike led E. A. (Bob) Montgomery to the site. Montgomery staked the mine and drove a tunnel a few hundred feet in length, which revealed a gold vein almost as long. Visitors to the mine—such as George Graham Rice—were awestruck by the discovery and proclaimed it as great a discovery as the Mohawk in Goldfield. Montgomery sold the mine to eastern steel tycoon Charles Schwab for a reported $5 million. Schwab built a 200-ton cyanide plant to process the ore. But the Montgomery-Shoshone never lived up to expectations. The vein proved to be shallow, although it did produce some $1.4 million over three years. [NHS]

280. RIEPETOWN. Located in White Pine County, 4 miles SW of Ely. Riepetown was a wide-open town, catering to the miners who worked in the company towns of Ruth, McGill, and Kimberly. It was a conglomeration of saloons, sporting houses, dance halls, gambling dens, and had a reputation for being one of the wildest towns in Nevada. Street brawls, general mayhem, and occasional gunplay were commonplace. Public outrage forced a county grand jury investigation, and county officials refused to renew saloon licenses in the town. Riepetown countered by incorporating the town and issued its own licenses. In 1914 the town was a refuge for I. W. W. (Wobbly) agitators, and even elected one as Mayor. Prohibition finally forced Riepetown into submission, and it gradually faded into obscurity. [NHS]

281. ROCHESTER. Located in Pershing County, 24 miles NE of Lovelock. This photo shows the camp of East Rochester, *circa* 1912, during the boom period. A building is under construction at lower right, two more are framed and going up at left. Tents dot the landscape in the distance. Supplies are stacked in the street. Leases for mines were bought and sold with a kind of frenzy, and work and revelry went on around the clock. Lumber and goods were brought in by freight wagon and motorized truck. East Rochester was located at the base of the mountain nearly two miles from the original camp of Rochester. The most popular social center in all the Rochester camps was Dreamland, a dance hall that opened in 1915 with a gala "Mule Skinner's Ball," complete with an eight-piece orchestra. [NHS]

282. ROCHESTER. Rich silver float was discovered here in June, 1912 by Joseph F. Nenzel.
Working on a grubstake, Nenzel by himself shipped out a load of ore that assayed $73 a ton.
When he shipped out a second load, word leaked out of a rich new strike. Nenzel was persuaded
to give a lease on Nenzel Hill to a group of investors, and this became known as the Big Four Lease.
Almost at once, as soon as the ground was worked, the main ore body was struck. The resulting boom
brought thousands into the district, and in less than two months, three separate camps had been established.[JG]

283. ROCHESTER. Photograph by N. E. Johnson, *circa* 1913, of mules hauling timbers to the mines,
with a partial view of East Rochester in the background. There were two other Rochester camps, called
"Upper Camp," and "Lower Camp." Upper Camp was the largest of the two, boasting a newspaper, hotel,
stores, and saloons. In 1914 the Nevada Short Line Railroad built a spur line into the district. In 1915 a
100-ton capacity mill was in operation, and in 1917 an aerial tramway was constructed to carry ore to the
mill at Lower Rochester. [PE]

284. ROCHESTER. "First two-story building, Rochester." Photo by William E. Moore, Winnemucca, Nevada, who made a series of Rochester photo cards in 1913, only one year after Joseph Nenzel's discovery. Production continued in the district into the 1920's but declined thereafter, with sporadic activity until the onset of World War II. Rochester today is the site of a huge open-pit mine operated by Coeur D'Alene Mining Company and is one of the largest silver producers in Nevada. [RONL]

285. ROUND MOUNTAIN. Located in Nye County, 60 miles N of Tonopah. A rich strike was made here in the spring of 1906. Later, extensive placer deposits were found, and a five-mile long flume was built to bring water to the ground so that it could be worked with hydraulic monitors. This card is post-marked June, 1907 and shows a mixture of tents and wooden buildings, with a wide Main Street. Unlike many mining towns, which soon became ghost towns, Round Mountain has had a long life due to its extensive deposits of low-grade ores. Except for the period during World War II, mining has been almost continuous. Even today, there is an open-pit mine here, one of the largest in the nation, with annual reserves estimated at $150 million. [RG]

286. ROUND MOUNTAIN. Message on card reads: "Here's a picture of the camp I'm making my home at the present time. I can't help but be good here for there's no place to dissipate. Have a splendid job. Am always through by noon. Am doing pastry and bread at the Tarbell Hotel." The Tarbell Hotel was owned by Fred Tarbell and advertised as a "new and first-class hotel." The mines at Round Mountain received much attention from the mining press of the day, and shares could be purchased on any mining exchange in Nevada or California. The Round Mountain gold mine today has removed most of the original Round Mountain and the pit occupies the old red-light district, also known as "Sunnyside." [NHS]

287. ROUND MOUNTAIN. Date of this card is *circa* 1909. The property of the Round Mountain Mining Company, the leading producer in the district, comprised 350 acres acquired in 1906. From1906-1913 it produced $2 million in gold, out of which it paid $328 thousand in dividends. The ore averaged between $6 and $10 a ton, but owing to the large ore bodies, costs were low. The main shaft was sunk to a level of 900 feet and had more than seven miles of underground workings. A large amount of gold had also been produced by working placer ground on company property below the outcrop of the big vein. [RONL]

288. ROUND MOUNTAIN. "Cleaning Bed Rock, Round Mountain, Nev." Part of the hydraulic mining operation, showing a portion of the pipe that carried water to operate the monitors. The monitor was constructed much like a fire-hose nozzle (but usually much larger) and could direct a stream of water under high pressure with tremendous force. Ore-bearing earth could be moved in large quantities, even an entire hillside. When bedrock was reached, a crew went over the ground looking for nuggets and particles of gold. [MK]

289. RUBY HILL. Located in Eureka County, 2 miles W of Eureka. The caption at bottom of card reads: "Eureka Con. Mine. Ruby Hill, Nev." On back of card is written: "The famous Ruby Hill Mine at Eureka Dec. 20, 1909." In 1908 the Eureka Consolidated had merged with the Richmond Mine and mill to form one company, Richmond & Eureka Consolidated. The construction of this large plant had been completed in 1907-08. From the 1870's on, this mine was one of the great silver producers in Nevada, having its own short-line railroad, the Ruby Hill Railroad, end of track at Eureka, two miles distant. [RG]

290. RUTH. Located in White Pine County, 5 miles NW of Ely. This view shows the extensive copper mining facilities as they appeared *circa* 1919. Ore was discovered here in 1900 and explorations by the Nevada Consolidated Copper Company resulted in full scale operations by 1904. At first, mining was done underground, through shafts and stopes, but in 1907 steam shovels began working in an open-pit. The Liberty Pit, as it came to be known, was eventually enlarged more than a mile long, over half a mile wide, and one thousand feet deep. It was considered one of the largest open-pit mines in the world. Today the dumps and remaining ores are processed for gold. [RG]

29l. RUTH. This photo shows the buildings of the company town, used to house and feed workers. By 1920 Ruth had a population of some 900 people. The company provided a boarding house for single men, a commissary, hospital, and housing for men with families, utilities provided for. Some of the buildings used to house employees can be seen in the foreground. As the area of the Liberty Pit was continually expanding, these buildings had to be moved and relocated to a site called New Ruth in 1955. [RG]

292. RUTH. This photo shows the commissary of the Nevada Consolidated Copper Company, *circa* 1918. The reverse writing at bottom of card reads: "View of dining room, Star Pointer boarding house. Ruth, Nevada." The town had a telephone exchange, the Ruth Photo Play Company (a motion picture house, and a novelty for a mining town), and several saloons, which were not owned or operated by Nevada Consolidated Copper Company. There was stage service three times weekly to Eureka, fare $10. [RONL]

293. RUTH. By 1908 a summer baseball league had been organized in White Pine County. Each company town had its own team: Ruth, McGill, Ely, Copper Flat, and one representing the Nevada Northern Railroad. Teams were sponsored by the copper companies, who bought uniforms and donated land for the baseball diamond. [ROGL]

294. SCHURZ. Located in Mineral County, 36 miles E of Yerington. The town of Schurz was headquarters for the Walker Lake Indian Reservation, largely composed of Paiute Indians. In 1869 each Indian family was given forty acres of land along the Walker River, with water rights, where there was unclaimed range land. This was supplemented with additional lands in the Pyramid Lake Indian Reservation in the same year. Caption on card reads: "Piute [sic] War Dance, Schurz, Nev." [RG]

295. SCHURZ. A view of the railroad depot at left, an engine of the Nevada & California Railroad, and the Nevada Mercantile Store, *circa* 1908. Schurz was originally a station on the Carson & Colorado Railroad, which was acquired in 1905 by Southern Pacific and renamed the Nevada and California Railroad. [PE]

296. SCHURZ. An advertising card for Miller & Company, which ran automobile stages to Rawhide in 1909. Schurz was a station on the Southern Pacific Railroad and its proximity to Rawhide (some 41 miles due east) made it the closest rail stop. Passengers would leave the train at Schurz and take whatever means of transportation they could get, usually an auto stage, sometimes a conventional stage. The railroad depot is at extreme right. Among the passengers eager to leave for the bumpy ride to Rawhide are several ladies, one holding a parasol. [RG]

297. SEARCHLIGHT. Located in Clark County, 50 miles SW of Las Vegas. The Searchlight Mining District was organized in July, 1898. By 1902 the town was booming, and the local newspaper, the *Searchlight*, was boosting its advantages. In 1907, at its peak, there was a population of some 3,000. That same year the Barnwell & Searchlight Railroad was completed, with connections at Barnwell, California, with the Santa Fe line. The boom faded later that year as profitable ore bodies were almost exhausted. The principal mines in the district were the Quartette and Duplex, which produced over $3 million in gold and silver. [RG]

298. SEARCHLIGHT. This photo is *circa* 1910 and caption reads: "Looking east on Hobson Street, Searchlight, Nev." Louis W. Godin's general merchandise store is at right. Though the town had declined in population to only 300 at this time, it had a newspaper, electric power, three railroad agents, a telephone exchange, shoe cobbler, two ice and cold storage plants, an auto stage with tri-weekly service, public school, Wells Fargo agent, telegraph office, saloons, mining recorder, and railroad depot. By this time, however, Searchlight had seen better days. Most of the large mines had run out of ore and mining was left to lessees and independents. [RONL]

299. SEARCHLIGHT. An interesting photo showing a doubles tennis match on a court built adjacent to a mine, *circa* 1908. Note the ore car in the background, and at left the large roller used to pack the surface of the court. The juxtaposition of sport and mining here is proof that life in a mining town had its amenities, and shows how resourceful people can be in providing for those pleasures. [PE]

300. SEARCHLIGHT. Card is postmarked April 30, 1912 and shows the office of the Searchlight Telephone Company. The switchboard can be seen to the left of the cash register. By 1910 most mining towns had their own independent telephone companies, and a few—Tonopah, Goldfield, Austin and Ely—issued directories to subscribers. Even some smaller camps had telephone connections, and some distant mines, such as the Mary Mine and the Betty O'Neal. [RONL]

301. SEVEN TROUGHS. Located in Pershing County, 28 miles NW of Lovelock. An early photo card, *circa* 1907 by H. Lee Jellum, just as the boom was getting started in this district. Note there are no mill buildings in this view, only an assortment of tents that outline the shape the town would take. The Kindergarten Mill does not appear, nor the Seven Troughs Hotel, both landmarks built later, in 1910-11. On March 7, 1908 the *Seven Troughs Miner* announced the Kindergarten Mine had reportedly found ore running $100,000 a ton, so rich it was called "jewelry gold," and was stored for safekeeping in the bank vault at nearby Vernon. The district produced $3.2 million through 1940; though the assays ran very high, the ore deposits were small. [RG]

302. SEVEN TROUGHS. Another view of the town, *circa* 1911, looking west, made by Osborn Photo. At far left is the mill of the Kindergarten Mine erected in 1911. In the center of the view is the two story Seven Troughs Hotel, and to the left of it the Coney Island Club. Scattered among the wood frame buildings are a number of tents and tent-structures with wooden foundations. [PE]

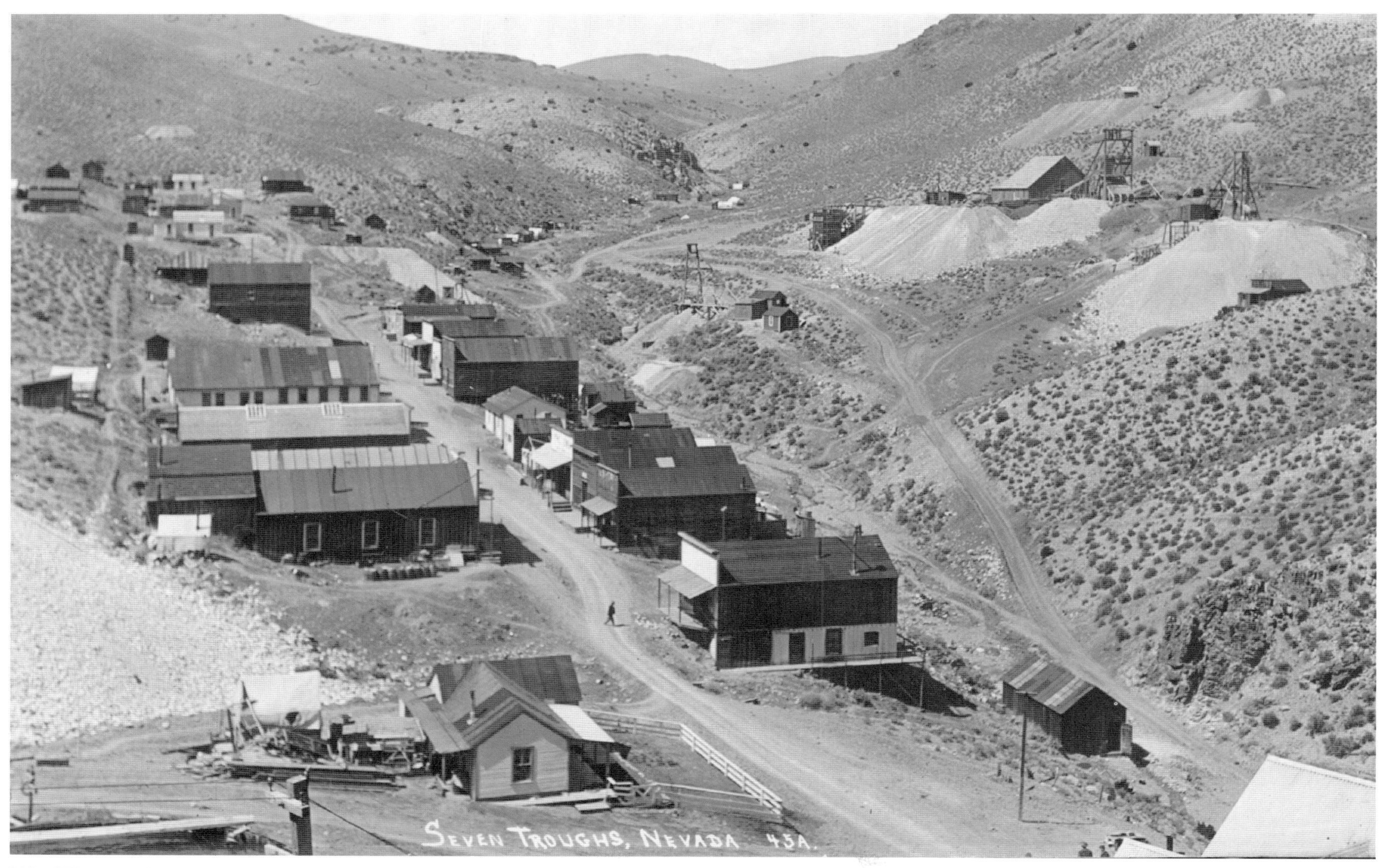

303. SEVEN TROUGHS. This view was taken from the site of the Kindergarten Mill (not shown here), looking east. There were four camps in the Seven Troughs Mining District: Seven Troughs, Mazuma, Vernon and Farrell. There was friendly rivalry between the camps, played out on the baseball diamond, or in trying to outdo one another in a Fourth of July celebration, or drilling contest. Labor Day celebrations were always held at Seven Troughs, however, at the Kindergarten Mine, and people from all four camps would gather there for an outdoor picnic that one newspaper said featured two whole steers, gallons of beans, barrels of coffee, and four hundred loaves of bread. [RONL]

304. SILVER CITY. Located in Lyon County, near Gold Hill and Virginia City. This card is postmarked March 2, 1903. The photograph was taken when the bottom portion of the view was in shade, probably late afternoon, and shows the road leading from Devil's Gate at lower left. Silver City was an important town in the Comstock, site of the Grosh brothers discovery in 1853-7. It rivaled Virginia City and Gold Hill during the bonanza days, not for its mines, but because it was on the main road between the Comstock and the Carson River mills. It was also an important center for its quartz mills. [PE]

305. SILVER CITY. This card is postmarked Silver City, November 19, 1908. A post office was established here in territorial days, May 10, 1860. In this view, taken from a slope overlooking the town, Main Street is clearly visible. The large building in the center with the tower-like facade is the Catholic Church. [RG]

306. SILVER CITY. The Overman Mine was one of the earliest producers on the lower Comstock, and through 1940 had yielded $2.5 million in silver and gold. By 1874 it had reached a depth of 1,150 feet and was still producing in 1882, when miners in the Exchequer Mine struck an underground cavern of hot water which flooded the Overman, Crown Point, Yellow Jacket, and other mines. Work at the Overman ceased, except for occasional working of the upper levels from which low-grade ore was taken. In 1890 the Gold Hill Pumping Association was formed, and thirteen mines spent $650 thousand in a fruitless effort to lower water levels. The Overman Mill, not affected by the flooding, continued to process ore for other mines. [RONL]

307. SILVER CITY. This card is postmarked Silver City, dated September 16, 1903, and was made by the Nevada Photo Company, of Virginia City. The McTigue Mill was located near the south edge of Silver City and processed low-grade ores from the Comstock. Note the crude smelting furnace and short chimney just to the right of the mill. [PE]

308. SILVER PEAK. Located in Esmeralda County, 30 miles SW of Tonopah. Situated in the lowest part of Clayton Valley, this area was first settled in territorial days, and the Silver Peak Mining District was organized February 1, 1865. In 1906 the Silver Peak Railroad was completed and trains began running to Blair, with connections to Tonopah and Goldfield, via Blair Junction. A fire swept the town in 1948 and destroyed much of the business section, but activity in the district continues with the mining of lithium and salt deposits. [RG]

309. SMELTER. Located in White Pine County, 8 miles N of East Ely. The sender of this card wrote: "We send this to show where we live, in the last house in last row marked X." The name of this place was originally McGill, but was changed to Smelter from September 7, 1907 until August 14, 1908, when it again reverted to McGill. The townsite was originally on land known as the McGill Ranch, owned by William N. McGill, who had worked in the 1870's in White Pine County as a surveyor for the U. S. government. [DAVE]

310. SMELTER. This view shows the smelter and concentrator plant with the elevated trestle for hauling ore at right of view. In 1922 the entire mill and trestle were destroyed by fire. A new mill was built the following year to process concentrates from Ely, and operated until the 1980's. The tall smokestack, which had been the tallest structure in Nevada when it was built, was imploded in 1994. [NHS]

311. SODAVILLE. Located in Mineral County, 4 miles S of Mina. The Silver Dyke properties at Sodaville were tungsten producers, and the mill shown here was built *circa* 1928. Earlier, Sodaville had been an important division point on the Carson & Colorado Railroad. In 1900-01, during the Tonopah boom, and before any railroad lines had been built south to Tonopah, freight was hauled the long distance by horses and mules. But in 1904, when the railroad to Tonopah was completed, Sodaville lost its status as a freight forwarding center. [JJ]

312. SPARKS. Located in Washoe County, 2.5 miles E of Reno. Ladies in white dresses with picture hats and parasols turned out for this Labor Day celebration, *circa* 1907. Dignitaries in the shade of a gazebo listen to a speaker address the crowd. Incorporated in 1905, the town was named in honor of John Sparks, who was Governor of Nevada at the time. The town, with a large railroad payroll, had several general merchandise stores, hotels, professional men, bakery, electric interurban service to Reno, two newspapers, real estate agents, meat market, Wells Fargo agent, schools, and two Chinese laundries. [PE]

313. SPARKS. This card shows a trolley of the Reno Traction Company, which provided service between Reno and Sparks. Service began in 1906 and continued until September, 1927. In the early days it was used by employees of the Southern Pacific who worked at the railroad shops in Sparks but lived in Reno. There was also a competing line, Nevada Interurban. When automobiles and bus service came into use, the lines were no longer profitable, and service was discontinued.
[RONL]

314. SPARKS. View shows the railroad engine shop buildings at right. In 1904 Sparks became the new division point on the Southern Pacific Railroad when facilities were moved from Wadsworth. The new facilities cost $1.5 million, complete with electric cranes, and the roundhouse had stalls for forty engines. Repairs were also made to rolling stock. The shops employed some 600 workers, with a monthly payroll of over $100,000. In 1907 Sparks had a population of 2,000. [ROGL]

315. SPARKS. John Sparks, a Democrat, was Governor of Nevada, 1903-1908. He was in office during the labor troubles in Goldfield, and in 1907, at the urging of George Wingfield, requested federal troops be sent into Goldfield. Governor Sparks had appeared in Goldfield and Tonopah on several occasions, sometimes in the company of Diamondfield Jack Davis, who acted as bodyguard for George Wingfield. Sparks was a rancher and cattleman before entering politics. He owned a large ranch called "the Alamo" between Carson City and Reno where he raised prize Herefords, as well as elk and buffalo. The city of Sparks was named for him. [JG]

316. STAR POINTER. Located in White Pine County, 1.5 miles S of Ruth. The Star Pointer copper mine was one of the largest producers in the district, located between the Liberty Pit and the Kimberly Pit. A spur line of the Nevada Central Railroad to Star Pointer was completed August 16, 1907. [JG]

317. STEAMBOAT SPRINGS. Located in Washoe County, 11 miles S of Reno. Mark Twain described the springs (or geysers) in 1863: "From one spring the boiling water is ejected a foot or more by the infernal force at work below, and in the vicinity of all of them one can hear a constant rumbling and surging, somewhat resembling the noises peculiar to a steamboat in motion, hence the name." This photo card gives an interesting view of U. S. Highway 395 as it appeared *circa* 1920. [FH]

318. STEWART. Located in Ormsby County, 3.5 miles S of Carson City. An early view of the Indian School, before the construction of buildings built of native stone. The school was established in 1901 and named for Senator William M. Stewart, who was instrumental in its founding. The school accepted young Indians of the Paiute, Shoshone, and Washoe tribes. Vocational classes included stock raising, farming, carpentry, blacksmithing, printing and bookbinding, and various mechanical skills. Many of its graduates achieved success in these fields. The entire school was closed in 1980 and its students absorbed into the public school system in Ormsby County. Today one of the buildings is used to display native crafts and artifacts. Others are used by Western Nevada Community College. [DOUG]

319. STRAWBERRY. Located in White Pine County, in the Newark Valley, 30 miles NE of Eureka. A Fourth of July parade on Main Street, complete with a brass band, decorated float pulled by two horses, a crowd of spectators, and several automobiles. Strawberry was a small and remote agricultural and ranching community, and when this photograph was taken, *circa* 1912, had a population of no more than 60. It had a post office active from September 7, 1899 until November 30, 1938, and stage connections semi-weekly with Cold Creek, fare $3.00, and with Eureka, fare $2.00. [PE]

320. SUTRO. Located in Lyon County, 5 miles E of Dayton. Adolph Sutro conceived the idea of a tunnel to drain and ventilate the mines on the Comstock Lode. Work on the project began in 1869 and connection with the Savage Mine was made in 1878. The town of Sutro was platted with broad avenues, shops, residences, and a newspaper, *The Sutro Independent* . Sutro himself built an elaborate Victorian mansion in the townsite. He moved to San Francisco in 1879 and was later elected mayor of that city. View shows entrance to the tunnel, workmen in foreground. Card has an undivided back, prior to 1908. [ROGL]

321. SWEETWATER. When this photograph was made in 1910, the Sweetwater school had six students and one teacher. The settlement was originally a stage station on the road to Aurora in the early 1860's. At the turn of the century, Sweetwater was an agricultural community with a hotel and general store. The 1910 census lists a population of 150. The post office opened in 1870 and was discontinued in 1925. [PE]

322. THISBE. Located in Washoe County, 7 miles W of Wadsworth. This was a non-agency station on the Southern Pacific Railroad. In 1925 a cloudburst washed out part of the track. Photograph shows many laborers and a mechanized shovel at work repairing the roadbed and track. [ROGL]

323. TONKIN. Located in Eureka County, 60 miles NW of Eureka. An agricultural and ranching community named for John G. Tonkin, who was the first postmaster in the settlement. A post office was established December 9, 1898 and discontinued March 14, 1931. The 1910 census lists a population of 30. [PE]

324. THOMPSON. Located in Lyon County, 12 miles N of Yerington. A view of the copper smelter of the Mason Valley Mines Company, which commenced operation in 1912. Ore was brought here on the Nevada Copper Belt Railroad. A small community formed around the plant, with a general store, hotel, saloons, dentist, and physician. Population in 1912 was 400. The smelter operated intermittently through 1928, when it closed permanently. A post office served he community from June 11, 1911 until June, 1920. [JG]

325. TOBAR. Located in Elko County, 16 miles SSE of Wells. Originally a station on the Western Pacific Railroad, a townsite was laid out in 1913, when the area was promoted as affording great opportunities for dry farming. View shows the town, *circa* 1914. Sign on the building at lower center reads: "Clover Mercantile Co." On back of card is written: "James M. Bassford. Tobar." By 1916 there was a newspaper, the *Sentinel*, a school, hotel, two mercantile stores, and post office. In 1918 the name was changed to Clover City, and in 1921 back again to Tobar. Several dry years and short growing seasons dashed the hopes of farmers who had been lured by extravagant land promotions, and the town went into permanent decline in the 1920's. [JJ]

326. TONOPAH. County seat of Nye County. Discovered in 1900 by James L. Butler, the town was originally named Butler, but changed to Tonopah in 1905. It was the site of Nevada's second great silver bonanza. Tonopah would become one of the great mining centers of the early twentieth century, complete with a stock exchange, a large railroad center, banks, hotels, newspapers, schools, opera house, library, electric, telephone and water systems. When mining ceased at the beginning of World War II, production had reached $149 million. Date of this card is *circa* 1907. [RG]

327. TONOPAH. A partial view of the silver mines at Tonopah, *circa* 1905-06, with part of the town in the foreground. Production of the mines continued to rise each year, reaching a peak during the period 1910-14, when the annual yield averaged $8.5 million. Some of the richest mines in the district were the Mizpah, Desert Queen, Montana, Tonopah Extension, Tonopah Mining Company, Tonopah-Belmont, West End, Halifax, Gypsy Queen, etc. The West End and Halifax were both properties of F. M. "Borax" Smith, who also owned the Tonopah & Tidewater Railroad. [RG]

328. TONOPAH. The famous Thomas Flyer pauses briefly in Tonopah, surrounded by a crowd of spectators. The route of the New York to Paris automobile race in 1908 took the cars and their drivers through Nevada: Ely to Tonopah, Goldfield to Rhyolite, then on to California. The Thomas Flyer shown here at left, a 60-horsepower car with a chain drive, won the race. This car was later owned by Bill Harrah of Reno, and for many years was on display in Harrah's Automobile Museum. Today the car is part of the permanent display in the National Automobile Museum, Reno. [JG]

329. TONOPAH. Not nearly as famous as the Gans-Nelson championship fight at Goldfield in 1906, the Gans-Herman fight was an attempt to repeat the success of the Goldfield contest. This card was issued to advertise the fight in Tonopah, which was sponsored by the Casino Athletic Club. The purse was $20,000 and for the light heavyweight championship title. Gans was the champion, Herman the challenger. Gans won the fight in the eighth round. Rex Beach wrote a colorful account of this fight, which appeared in *Everybody's Magazine*, pp. 464-474, 1907. [RONL]

330. TONOPAH. The idea for the Tonopah Public Library originated with Mrs. Hugh Brown and the wives of professional men at Tonopah. Charles Knox and Mr. Parkhurst of the Montana Mine took an interest in the project and donated $1,000 and a lot on Mineral Street. Additional funds were raised through a book social and a minstrel show at the Opera House. The ladies collected several thousand books and funds for magazine subscriptions. The little stone building was erected with additional funds from the Mine Operators' Association. [RONL]

331. TONOPAH. The Fourth of July may have been the most celebrated community event in mining town social life. The highlight of festivities was always a colorful parade. People dressed in special costumes decorated with stars and stripes, some as Uncle Sam, some as Miss Liberty. The Tonopah Boys' Marching Band turned out for the occasion, neatly dressed (even wearing neckties), posing for their photograph in a patriotic card dated 1907. [JG]

332. TONOPAH. By 1914 the Tonopah Fire Department was fully motorized. At left is the chief's car. In the middle is a Seagrave ladder-equipped engine. The engine at right is also a Seagrave and may have been fitted with a chemical or conventional tank. Note the row of portable chemical extinguishers mounted on the side of the middle engine. Also note the ten firemen wearing helmets and waterproof coats. [PE]

333. TONOPAH. A baseball game between Tonopah and Goldfield, August 22, 1909. Each town had its own baseball team, and there were also teams representing fraternal organizations. Teams usually played against neighboring teams, although on occasion a team would board a train and play a game in some more distant town. Baseball, boxing, and a horseracing track offered considerable variety to sports fans, as well as trap-shooting, broom ball, and auto racing in the desert. [JG]

334. TRANSVAAL. Located in Nye County, 15 miles NE of Beatty. "Transvaal, Nev., two weeks old," photo by A. E. Holt, of Rhyolite, Nevada, April, 1906. Gold was discovered here in late March, 1906 and a rush brought several hundred people. By June, the rush had reached its peak and when the shallow deposits had been worked out the camp died a quick death, having lasted only three months. It may have been the shortest-lived camp in the entire Bullfrog Mining District. Transvaal was truly a flash in the pan. [NHS]

335. TUNGSTONIA. Located in White Pine County, 45 miles NE of Ely. Photo shows the crew of the Glencoe Mine, *circa* 1917. The man at left, arms folded across his chest, is identified as A. P. Ryan. Tungsten was discovered here in 1910, and in 1915 a mill was built to process ore. The metal was much in demand during World War I, but when the war ended the price fell sharply and the camp was abandoned. A post office operated here for only seven months in 1917. [DAVE]

336. TUSCARORA. Located in Elko County, 45 miles NW of Elko. This rare photograph of Weed Street is *circa* 1905 and shows the Idaho Saloon at left and A. V. Lancaster's general merchandise store. Population of this once-booming town had declined to 350 by 1907, and to 300 by 1910. Production of the mines had dropped steadily since 1885 and by 1900 nearly all had closed. Tuscarora had been eclipsed by southern Nevada's mining boom. In 1904 the mines were reorganized into a new company and an effort to work low-grade ores proved unsuccessful. Total production for the period 1870 through 1940 was $9.4 million. By 1920 the town would virtually be abandoned. Today it is the site of an active artists community and a modern open-pit gold mine. [RONL]

337. TUSCARORA. This bird's-eye view of Tuscarora is *circa* 1905, when the town was in decline. Earlier it had been one of Nevada's largest producers of gold and silver, with a peak population of some 4,000. Tuscarora had a large Chinese population, a district known as "Little Shanghai," complete with joss houses and opium dens. At the height of its prosperity it was the largest town in central Nevada. At the right where the writer of this card has placed an "X" is the Tuscarora school. The writer has mistakenly exaggerated the gold production figures. These Tuscarora photo cards were mailed by the same person, whose handwritten comments appear on both cards. [RG]

338. UNIONVILLE. Located in Pershing County, 25 miles S of Mill City. Unionville had its beginnings in 1862, when rich ore was discovered. For a time it was called Dixie, until Union sympathizers gained the upper hand and named the town Unionville. Mark Twain was one of the many hopefuls who tried his hand at mining here, but after three weeks of driving a tunnel he left, having failed to strike it rich. The Arizona Mill, shown here in a photo taken in 1909 (long after it had ceased production), was discovered in 1868. By 1874 it was one of the richest properties in the district, worked by sixty to seventy miners. From 1872 to 1878 the Arizona Mine yielded close to $5 million. [JJ]

339. VERDI. Located in Washoe County, 10 miles W of Reno. The building at right is the Verdi Bakery, and next to it the building with the belfry is the Catholic Church. This view is *circa* 1912. Population at this time was 300. The principal business was the Verdi Lumber Company, with its large sawmills and box-making plant. Verdi was a sub-station of the Reno Power, Light & Water Company. The town had a public school, telephone exchange, telegraph office, Wells Fargo Agency, hotel, physician, and railroad depot. [RONL]

340. VERDI. A panorama view, *circa* 1912, showing the business district at bottom, and at lower center, the depot and track of the Southern Pacific Railroad. One of the most famous train robberies in Nevada history happened at Verdi on November 5, 1870, when Chat Roberts and his gang broke into the express car and seized a gold shipment. This was accomplished by detaching the express car from the rest of the train. The robbers were subsequently caught and given long prison terms. [PE]

341. VERDI. Although Verdi had suffered serious fires several times—in 1902 when the box factory burned, in 1903 when an entire city block was destroyed, and another in 1908—the worst one occurred in 1916. A strong wind carried sparks from the lumber mill over the town, setting fires in several places. In less than an hour some forty-five homes were destroyed and many damaged. Loss was estimated at $1 million. This photo shows a portion of the burned district where homes and buildings burned to the ground. [PE]

342. VERNON. Located in Pershing County, 30 miles NW of Lovelock. An early view of the town, *circa* 1905 by Lee Jellum, who made many photo cards of towns and mines in the Seven Troughs Mining District. The town had been platted as a townsite early in 1905 and reached its zenith in 1907-08. Vernon became the financial center of the Seven Troughs District, with the only secure bank vault. Stages ran daily between the camps in this district, and twice daily to Lovelock, fare $3.00. [PE]

343. VERNON. This photo card is *circa* 1907. Vernon was one of four towns in the Seven Troughs Mining District. Population at this time was 600. The town was the commercial center for the district and boasted a stock exchange, bank, light and power company, telephone exchange, hotels, assay office, commercial club and saloons. Investors and speculators rushed into the district from as far away as Goldfield, but by 1910 the bloom was off the boom and the mines were closing down. During its peak years, Vernon had three newspapers: the *Vernon Miner, Vernon Review*, and the *Seven Troughs Miner*. But by 1914 the population of Vernon was down to a mere fifty people, and the newspapers had long since ceased publication. Most of the buildings at Vernon were either moved elsewhere to new locations or razed for salvage. [RONL]

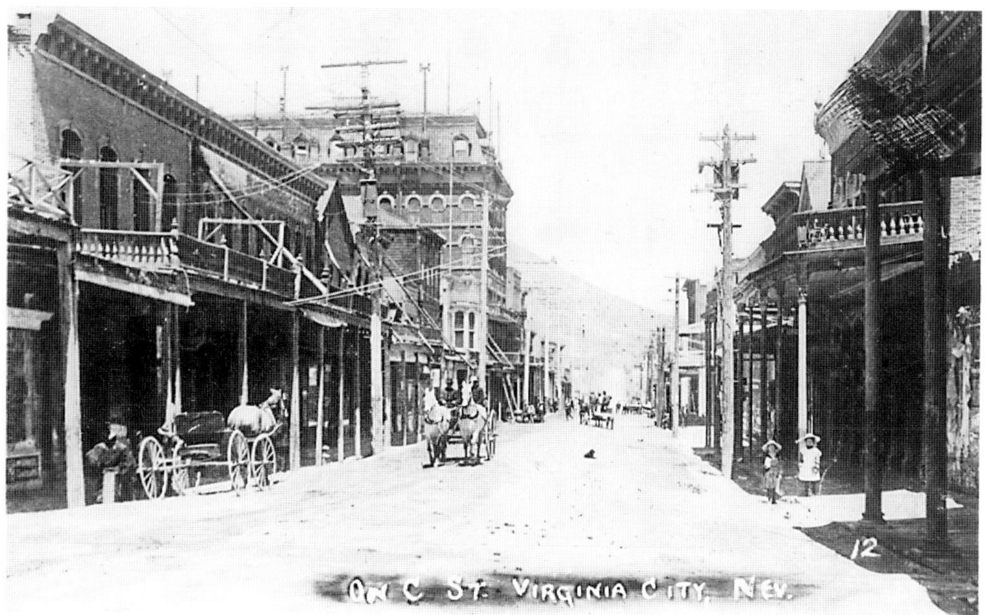

344. VIRGINIA CITY. County seat of Storey County. The scene of Nevada's longest and most spectacular mining boom. Mining began here in territorial days and continued until 1899, and irregularly thereafter. During the early 1870's Virginia City had a population of some 25,000 people, served by stores of all descriptions, four banks, six churches, private and public schools, five newspapers, a hospital, railroad, and many fraternal organizations. The large building at left with the mansard roof is the International Hotel. It was the most imposing building in Virginia City. Located at the corner of C and Union, it was six stories tall, serviced with an elevator, and had 162 rooms. On the ground floor was a handsomely furnished dining room and bar. Almost a quarter of a million dollars was spent on its construction. [RG]

345. VIRGINIA CITY. Date of this photo is *circa* 1909 and shows most of the central district of Virginia City. The photograph was taken from Cedar Hill, north of the town. The city still made an impressive appearance at this time, with many of the brick buildings that had been erected after the great fire of 1875 still in use. St. Mary's Church can be seen at left center, the Ophir and C & C Mines at lower left. The population in 1910 was 2,244. [RG]

346. VIRGINIA CITY. This street scene is *circa* 1905 and shows C Street in a somewhat neglected state. Wagons and buggies are present, but no automobiles. As evidenced by the utility poles, electricity and telephone service was available. The figure of a cast-iron Indian may be seen mounted on a pedestal in front of the barber shop. In 1905 there was still mining on the Comstock, but at a much reduced rate when compared to earlier days. The Consolidated Virginia, Ophir, Ward Shaft, Butters Plant, Union Mine, and others were still active. But Virginia City was in decline, and attention had focused upon the new mining boom to the south—Tonopah and Goldfield. [RONL]

347. VIRGINIA CITY. This photo shows the Fourth Ward School at right. Caption reads: "Pogonip. Virginia, Nev." Pogonip is a dense winter fog containing tiny ice crystals, from the Paiute and Shoshone, meaning "white death," feared by the Indians for causing pneumonia. The fog may be seen in this view extending in back of the school to the mountains in the distance. [RG]

348. VIRGINIA CITY. "Butters Plant, Virginia City, Nev." The Butters Tailings Mill was built in 1903 and used the latest methods in ore recovery. It was named for Charles Butters, who conceived the idea of re-working the tailings in Six Mile Canyon for gold and silver. In 1904 the Butters filter was introduced into the milling process, which proved very successful. The plant was modeled after South African cyanide plants and introduced many new features into milling low-grade ores. In 1907 ore shipped by rail from Tonopah was milled at the Butters Plant. [RONL]

349. VIRGINIA CITY. This photograph shows a Virginia & Truckee locomotive with train crew. A crew usually consisted of an engineer, fireman, brakeman, and conductor. Date of this card is *circa* 1905. The line between Carson City and Virginia City was completed in 1869. It was most active in the 1870's, when some thirty trains ran daily to handle the traffic, and at peak times, fifty trains a day would make the run. After 1900 the number of trains greatly decreased as production of the mines declined. [RONL]

350. WABUSKA. Located in Lyon County, 12 miles N of Yerington. A view of the railroad depot, *circa* 1912. Originally a station on the Carson & Colorado, then a station on the Oregon Short Line in 1908, Wabuska became a railroad center when the Nevada Copper Belt line was completed in 1911. It became the shipping point for the copper mines in the Mason Valley and for the smelter at Thompson. Population at this time was 100. The town had several stores, restaurant, boarding house, saloons, and a Wells Fargo Agency. Mining ceased after World War II and the town went into permanent decline. The Nevada Copper Belt Railroad went out of business in 1947. [NHS]

351. WABUSKA. Passenger service on the Nevada Copper Belt Railroad was never heavy, and so to accommodate light traffic, Hall-Scott motorized cars were used, powered by a gasoline engine. These cars could carry a full load of passengers and baggage, and were sometimes used to pull one or two freight cars. Date of this card is *circa* 1912, postmarked Wabuska. Passenger service over the line followed the route from Thompson to Wabuska, to Mason and Nordyke, and on occasion as far as Hudson and Ludwig. [PE]

352. WADSWORTH. Located in Washoe County, 32 miles E of Reno. This photo card is captioned: "Wadsworth Nev. 04." The card is signed "Linton," most probably W. D. Linton, who was a resident of Wadsworth. The depot was originally built by the old Central Pacific Railroad, later acquired by the Southern Pacific. Note the small plot of grass and fountain in the foreground. The large building in the background is the machine shop for the railroad. Wadsworth at this time was headquarters for the Truckee division of the line. The town was also an important freighting center for mining towns to the south. In 1904 Wadsworth lost its importance as a railroad center when Sparks was designated the new division point. [RG]

353. WADSWORTH. Message on front of card reads: "The last picture taken of the shop men in Wadsworth." Card is dated October 8, 1906. Relocation of the Southern Pacific Railroad shops from Wadsworth to Sparks had begun in 1904, when the railroad began moving equipment and buildings to Sparks. The railroad paid moving expenses and arranged transportation for all its employees. Demolition of the Wadsworth roundhouse commenced in December, 1904. To make matters worse for Wadsworth, the new main line bypassed Wadsworth several miles to the south, leaving the town without a rail connection. [PE]

354. WAHMONIE. Located in Nye County, 30 miles E of Beatty. A highly publicized silver discovery in 1928 at the old Hornsilver Mine sparked a small rush into the district. Like Weepah, Wahmonie was a camp of tents and automobiles, with speculators staking out mining claims in all directions. George Wingfield organized a mining company and financed exploration, but only small amounts of ore were ever shipped. But the excitement was short-lived, and Wahmonie was reclaimed by the desert. A post office was in service here from April 1, 1928 until April 30, 1929. It is appropriate that N. E. Johnson, who photographed so many Nevada boomtowns over a period of twenty years made this picture of Nevada's last boom camp. [JC]

How to Reach Walley Hot Springs: By railroad from Reno or Churchill to Carson; then by stage to Walley Hot Springs. Parties desiring to reach Springs can secure private conveyance by wiring to Springs from Reno or Churchill.

ANALYSIS OF WATER AT WALLEY HOT SPRINGS

	Grains per Gallon		Grains per Gallon
Silica	3.5924	Sodium Bicarbonate	8.3092
Iron and Aluminum Oxides	.3268	Magnesium Bicarbonate	.9741
Sodium Chloride	4.4365	Calcium Bicarbonate	4.4205
Sodium Sulphate	13.0875	Reported May 31, 1905, N. E. Wilson, State Chemist.	

NEVADA PRESS, CARSON CITY.

355. WALLEY HOT SPRINGS. Located in Douglas County, 3 miles SW of Genoa. This place was named for David and Harriet Walley, who first operated a spa here in 1862. Its thermal baths were popular with people suffering from arthritis and rheumatism. The springs flowed from a deep fault in the earth several hundred feet in length along the eastern slope of the Sierra Nevada from Walley to Jacks Valley, and on to Kirman Springs. In 1907-08 the property was owned and operated by M. L. Hewitt. Stages ran daily from Carson City. [RONL]

356. WEDEKIND. Located in Washoe County, 2 miles N of Sparks. "Arkell Mine, Wedekind District, near Reno, Nevada." Card is dated 1912. The district was named after George H. Wedekind, a piano tuner from Reno, who found gold here in 1896. In 1898 the Wedekind Mine began operations, producing some $100,000. Wedekind sold the mine to Governor John Sparks in 1901 for an even larger sum. Other mines in the district produced smaller amounts of ore. Briefly, from 1901-05, the camp was known as Wedekind, Bryan City, and Wedekind City. A post office was established in 1902 and discontinued in 1905. [ROGL]

357. WEEPAH. Located in Esmeralda County, 18 miles SW of Tonopah. One of the first to arrive at Weepah was N. E. Johnson, whose automobile and canvas sign appear in this photograph. Johnson did a series of spontaneous photo cards as well as stock-size photographs and panorama views. Also on the scene was a film crew from International Newsreel Company, of Los Angeles. They made a newsreel for distribution to theaters and a series of still photos for publication in newspapers. Weepah even had a "nightclub"— a large tent from which came the sound of laughing dancehall girls from Tonopah, dressed in evening gowns and dancing slippers, sipping champagne. [RG]

358. WEEPAH. Sometimes referred to as the last gold rush in Nevada, rich ore was found here in March, 1927. With the exception of about a dozen wooden buildings and tents, Weepah was mostly an automobile camp. People seeking their fortune had driven from all over the country to the new strike. They slept in their cars, cooked over campfires, bathed in laundry tubs, staked out claims in the desert around the clock, bought and sold leases at fever pitch. Five weeks after the strike, over 1,500 people had arrived. A year later the boom had fizzled and the place was almost deserted. [RG]

359. WEEPAH. Dining out in Weepah was strictly an informal affair, judging from the tent housing the "Weepah Cafe." The Weepah boom was sparked by the discovery of a shallow pocket of rich gold ore by two young men. Optimists believed if there was one such pocket there must surely be others. But despite all the fanciful publicity and digging in the surrounding desert, no others were found. [ROGL]

360. WELLS. Located in Elko County, 54 miles NE of Elko. A town first settled in 1869, and later a station on the Western Pacific and Southern Pacific. When the Nevada Northern Railroad built its line north from Ely, Wells had been hopeful it would become the northern terminus of the line. But Cobre won out, leaving the boosters in Wells disappointed. Date of this card is *circa* 1911. Population at this time was 700. Some of the signs visible are: C. A. Wiseman, garage; Wells Market; Mint Saloon; Newhouse Hotel, etc. [NHS]

361. WELLS. This card and the following pair form a panorama view of Wells, made by Long & Osborne, of Evanston, Wyoming, *circa* 1908. These cards were enclosed in an envelope and mailed, therefore not postmarked. However, the sender wrote descriptions and comments on the reverse side of each card. This card is the east end of Wells, showing a portion of the railroad yards, and at extreme right, a portion of the San Marin Hotel. [JG]

362. WELLS. On the reverse side of this card the sender wrote: "This is the western end. All I can see to admire are the mountains at the rear of town and they are beautiful and cold sometimes when covered with snow . . . The church you see is used seldom. Only in case of a funeral. I am sick to hear a good sermon." [JG]

363. WELLS. This card shows the central portion of town, the San Marin Hotel, A. W. Corle, general merchandise, a saloon, and the Bulls Head Hotel. The sender continued: "This shows the post office and the largest store here. It is narrow but powerful long. Like some of the heads around this place. This card shows all of Main Street and the other streets have no names. There are five saloons in this space." [JG]

364. WINNEMUCCA. County seat of Humboldt County. The town of Winnemucca is named for the famous Paiute Indian chief. In the early days the town was an important stage and freighting center, later a division point on the old Central Pacific Railroad. Today it is the commercial center of central Nevada, and the center of a large agricultural and stock grazing district. In the early part of the twentieth century it was a trading and freighting point for mining camps in the Spring City Mining District. This card is *circa* 1905 and shows the town before many permanent buildings had been constructed. The writer of this card has identified the express office, post office, and other places. [RG]

365. WINNEMUCCA. This bird's-eye view of the town, *circa* 1919, shows substantial buildings on both sides of Bridge Street. Several county buildings have been erected: a courthouse and jail, county hospital, and high school. An opera house costing $50,000 was a gift from U. S. Senator George S. Nixon. A modern water, electric power, and sewer system had been installed. Population had grown to 1,800. Winnemucca even had ambitions to become the new state capitol, replacing Carson City, but after a year of lobbying and collecting petitions, nothing came of the effort. [RG]

366. WINNEMUCCA. A freighting team and wagons headed for the mines, from a photograph taken before the turn of the century. Driving these heavy and cumbersome wagons was an art. The team usually was made up of mules and horses. The lead horse was trained to respond to a jerk line, and to know how far to circle out a turn so that the mules would follow the slack chain at just the right distance to negotiate the turn. The wheel horses held the weight of the wagons when the brakes were released. Each horse had a specific function, trained to respond to the lines held in the driver's hands, and those lines, depending upon the size of the team, might be as much as forty feet in length. [RONL]

367. WINNEMUCCA. Card is dated January 23, 1911. A. A. Wendell is listed in Polk's *Nevada Gazetteer* for 1914-15, as one of two dentists practicing in Winnemucca. Wendell is holding in his right hand a tooth extractor with a large tooth in its grip. Patients in those days were given gas as an anesthetic, called laughing gas (nitrous oxide) by lay persons. One presumably began laughing as soon as the gas was inhaled, which made a visit to the dentist seem not only painless but worth a good laugh. [DAVE]

368. WONDER. Located in Churchill County, 50 miles E of Fallon. This street scene is *circa* 1908 and shows a crowd gathered for a parade and celebration. At left is the Monarch Hotel, and next to it, James Holmes & Company store and saloon. The town was named for the Nevada Wonder Mine, discovered in April, 1906. A post office was opened in September, 1906 and closed in August, 1920. A railroad connecting Wonder and Fairview was proposed and a route was actually surveyed, but the necessary financing could not be raised and the line was never built. [RONL]

369. WONDER. This panorama view of Wonder is *circa* 1909. Gold quartz was found here in 1906 and hundreds rushed into the district. The town blossomed almost overnight. For a time, Wonder and Fairview (its neighbor to the south) were the focus of much excitement. Population in 1907- 08 was 1,500. The town had two newspapers, six mercantile stores, ten restaurants, several assay offices, two hotels, a bank, school, auto stage line, two laundries, a bath house, water works, and telephone connections with Fairview and Hazen. Several brokerage houses from Goldfield and Tonopah set up branch offices here, and stocks in Wonder's mines were traded on the exchanges at Tonopah and Goldfield. [RONL]

370. WONDER. Miners at the Nevada Wonder Mine pose for this photograph, *circa* 1912. Two miners can be seen standing in the cage at center, which took men to the lower depths of the mine. The Nevada Wonder commenced work in 1906 and operated until 1919. It was the principal mine in Wonder, one of the richest silver mines in Nevada, and produced $6.2 million through 1940. In 1912 the mill at Wonder was completed, operated by electric power brought by a transmission line over the Sierra Nevada from Bishop, California. When the mine closed in 1919, it spelled the end for Wonder. The post office closed in August, 1920, and the town was gradually abandoned. [NHS]

371. YERINGTON. County seat of Lyon County. At the turn of the century, Yerington was an agricultural and railroad town. It was originally named Greenfield after the fertile fields in the Mason Valley. The name was later changed to honor Henry M. Yerington, president of the Carson & Colorado Railroad. When plans were announced to build the Nevada Copper Belt Railroad through the Mason Valley, the citizens of Yerington raised $40,000 to help finance the line. But when the line was built, it skirted Yerington altogether, as railroad officials had believed that the town of Mason would become the largest city in Lyon County. [RG]

372. YERINGTON. "Parade, Second Section. Yerington. July 4th, 08." Yerington became the trading center for the Yerington Mining District in 1908, and when it became the county seat, the seat of local government. The mining district originally had been formed in the 1860's when prospectors found traces of silver, but the large copper deposits were unknown then. In those early days the mining district was called "Crazy Louse," and for a time was owned by Mark Twain, who said in later years that he never realized a penny out of it. [PE]

373. YERINGTON. Card is dated 1908. Sign at left reads: "John Deere, Studebaker Wagons and Buggies." The automobile had begun to replace the buggy, as evidenced in this photograph. In 1908 the county seat of Lyon County was still located in Dayton, thirty miles to the north. When a fire destroyed the Dayton courthouse in 1909, a bitter fight developed between Dayton and Yerington for the new courthouse. Yerington eventually won out and the new courthouse was built here. [RONL]

PHOTOGRAPHERS OF NEVADA REAL PHOTO POST CARDS, 1903-1928

(This list makes no claim to be complete. There are undoubtedly other makers of real photo cards not listed here. But it does represent those photographers who were most active in Nevada for the period 1903-1928. Dashes after the surname indicate a missing first name that could not be found in directories for the period. After the name of the photographer the place of business is given in parenthesis. Listed in the right-hand column are Nevada towns for which the photographer is known to have made cards.)

Allen Photo Company (Goldfield, Nevada)	Goldfield
Andrews, Wesley (Baker, Oregon)	Austin, Virginia City
Atherton & Son (Elko, Nevada)	Austin, Clifton, Elko, Winnemucca
Bertram, ———-.	Diamondfield, Goldfield
Booth, J. J. (Tonopah, Nevada)	Caliente, Manhattan, Tonopah
Brissell, ———-.	Tonopah
Busy Bee Photo	Wonder
Cann, William E. (Reno)	Reno, Virginia City
Dana, P. F. (San Francisco)	Reno
Dewitt, ———-.	Las Vegas
Down, ———-.	Goodsprings
Field, J. T. (Manhattan, Nevada)	Manhattan
Flessa, ———-.	Schurz
Foley, George	Round Mountain
Forbes, A. A.	Millers
Frashers (Pomona, California)	Many Nevada views, 1928 and later
Freeman, ——— .	Eureka, Palisade
Gallagher, C. D. (Ely, Nevada)	Copper Flat, Ely, Kimberly, McGill, Ruth Smelter
Giles, E. S.	Goldfield
Goepfert, ———.	Bannock
Haines, O. J.	Ruth
Ham, Rolly R.	Fallon
Heck, R. W. (Burns, Oregon)	McDermitt
Holt, A. Eugene (Rhyolite, Nevada)	Beatty, Bullfrog, Pioneer, Rhyolite, Transval
Jellum, H. Lee (Yreka, California)	Austin, Mazuma, Seven Troughs, Vernon

Johnson, N[ed] E. (Los Angeles and San Jose) — Divide, Hawthorne, Lucky Boy, Rawhide, Rochester, Weepah, Wahmonie

Judd, Oscar P. — Reno

Kelso, ——-. — Wonder

Kent, ——-. — Contact

Larson, P. Edward (Goldfield, Nevada) — Goldfield

Levitch, H. L. — Reno

Linton, W. D. (Wadsworth) — Olinghouse, Reno, Wadsworth

Long & Osborne (Evanston, Wyoming) — Battle Mountain, Contact, Wells

Mark, W. L. — Rhyolite

Marks, C. — Beatty

Martin, M. B. — Contact

Massie, ——-. — Metropolis

Mauz, J. (Fallon, Nevada) — Fallon

McClelland, ——-. — Bovard, Rawhide

Moore, William E. — Rochester, Winnemucca

Nevada Novelty Co. (Virginia City, Nevada) — Carson City, Virginia City

Nevada Photo Co. (Virginia City, Nevada) — Carson City, Virginia City

Oakes, Leon (Las Vegas, Nevada) — Las Vegas

Osborn Photo Co. — Lovelock, Virginia City

Osborn & Skinner (Tonopah, Nevada) — Belmont

Osborne, T. J. — Caliente, Pioche

Polin Brothers (Goldfield, Nevada) — Goldfield

Renbar, D. B. (Carson City, Nevada) — Carson City

Renear, ——-. — Carson City

Richards, ——-. — Gold Circle

Richardson, Guy H. (Wonder, Nevada) — Wonder

Shaw, B. F. (Virginia City, Nevada) — Virginia City

Sissons, ——. — Eureka

Smith, Albert L. (Carson City, Nevada) — Carson City

Smith, Alfred L. (Tonopah, Nevada) — Tonopah

Thyes & Reese — Reno

Welch & Tune (Goldfield, Nevada) — Columbia, Goldfield

Weyle, E. B. — Ely, Jarbidge, Tonopah

Wood, H. L. — McGill

PUBLISHERS OF PRINTED NEVADA POST CARDS, 1903-1928
(City in parenthesis is business location)

Albertype Company (New York City)

Allen Photo Company (Goldfield, Nevada)

American News Company (New York City)

Art Manufacturing Company (Amelia, Ohio)

Auburn Post Card Company (Auburn, Indiana)

C. A. Beemer (Sparks and Reno)

Richard Behrend (San Francisco)

Black & Ferguson (Fallon, Nevada)

Bobbe Lithograph Company (New York City)

A. C. Bosselman & Company (New York City)

Carson City Book & News Company (Carson City)

Clark & Secor, Publishers (Milwaukee)

Colorado News Company (Denver)

Dennison News Company (New York City)

Emporium Company (Carson City)

Grace B. Faxon, Publisher (Ely, Nevada)

The Goldfield News (Goldfield, Nevada)

Gray News Company (Salt Lake City)

J. N. Hall & Company (Blair, Nevada)

A. E. Holt, Publisher (Rhyolite, Nevada)

Tom Jones, Publisher (Cincinnati)

Arthur Knecht (Ely, Nevada)

S. Langsdorf & Company (New York City)

P. Edward Larson (Goldfield, Nevada)

Frank H. Leib, Publisher (Salt Lake City)

S. L. Mayer (Salt Lake City)

Miner's Drug Store (Tonopah, Nevada)

Edward H. Mitchell, Publisher (San Francisco)

Mott's Bazaar (Reno)

Nevada Novelty Company (Virginia City, Nevada)

Nevada Post Card Company (Goldfield, Nevada)

Newman Post Card Company (Los Angeles)

Pacific Novelty Company (San Francisco)

Pioneer Drug Store (Virginia City, Nevada)

Polin Brothers (Goldfield, Nevada)

Plunkett Brothers (Los Angeles)

Mrs. K. A. Raftice (Carson City)

Nelson Rounsevell, Publisher (Tonopah, Nevada)

C. R. Savage (Salt Lake City)

Carl F. Schader (Johnnie, Nevada)

J. Scheff & Brothers (San Francisco)

Shepard & Son (Reno)

Smith, Albert L. (Carson City)

St. Paul Souvenir Company (St. Paul)

A. A. Stafford (Carson City)

Curt Teich & Company (Chicago)

Vernon Tobler & Company (College Point, N. Y.)

William Tomkins, Publisher (Goldfield, Nevada)

Tribune Book & Stationery Store (Goldfield, Nevada)

M. F. Tucker (Elko, Nevada)

B. E. Walker (Ely, Nevada)

Welch & Tune (Goldfield, Nevada)

C. E. Wheelock & Company (Peoria, Illinois)

White & Company (Reno)

BIBLIOGRAPHY

Angel, Myron, ed. *History of Nevada, 1881.* [Originally published by Thompson & West.] Berkeley: Howell-North, 1958.

Beatty, Bessie, ed. *Who's Who in Nevada . . .* Los Angeles: Home Printing Company, 1907.

Brown, Mrs. Hugh. *Lady in Boomtown . . .* Palo Alto: American West Publishing Company, 1968.

Carlson, Helen S. *Nevada Place Names, a Geographical Dictionary.* Reno: University of Nevada Press, 1974.

Davis, Sam P. *The History of Nevada.* 2 volumes. Los Angeles: Elm Publishing Company, 1913.

Ellen, Mary, and Al Glass. *Touring Nevada. A Historic and Scenic Guide.* Reno: University of Nevada Press, 1983.

Elliott, Russell R. *Nevada's Twentieth-Century Mining Boom.* Reno and Las Vegas: University of Nevada Press, 1966.

Frickstad, W. N., and E. W. Thrall. *A Century of Nevada Post Offices*, 1852-1957. Oakland: Pacific Roto-Printing Company, 1958.

Gamett, James, and Stanley W. Paher. *Nevada Post Offices, an Illustrated History.* Las Vegas: Nevada Publications, [n.d.]

Glasscock, C. B. *Gold In Them Hills.* Indianapolis: Bobbs-Merrill Company, 1932.

Grover, David H. *Diamondfield Jack. A Study in Frontier Justice.* Norman: University of Oklahoma Press, 1985.

Johnston, Hank. *Death Valley Scotty . . .* Corona Del Mar: Trans-Anglo Books, 1974.

Lingenfelter, Richard E. *The Newspapers of Nevada.* San Francisco: John Howell Books, 1964.

Mack, Effie Mona. *Nevada, a History of the State . . .* Glendale: Arthur H. Clark Company, 1936.

Morgan, Hal, and Andreas Brown. *Prairie Fires and Paper Moons*; *the American Photographic Postcard . . .* Boston: David R. Godine, 1981.

Morris, Henry Curtis. *Desert Gold and Total Prospecting.* [Washington, D. C.] The Author, 1955.

Murbarger, Nell. *Ghosts of the Glory Trail.* Palm Desert, Cal.: Desert Magazine Press, 1956.

Murbarger, Nell. *Sovereigns of the Sage.* Palm Desert, Cal.: Desert Magazine Press, 1958.

Myrick, David F. *Railroads of Nevada and Eastern California.* 2 volumes. Reno and Las Vegas: University of Nevada Press, 1992.

Paher, Stanley W. *Las Vegas: As it Began—As it Grew.* Las Vegas: Nevada Publications, 1971.

Paher, Stanley W. *Nevada Ghost Towns and Mining Camps.* Berkeley: Howell-North, 1970.

Patterson, Edna B., Louise A. Ulph, and Victor Goodwin. *Nevada's Northeast Frontier.* Reno and Las Vegas: University of Nevada Press, 1991.

R. L. Polk & Company. *Nevada State Gazetteer and Business Directory, 1907-1908.* Salt Lake City: Century Printing Company, 1907.

R. L. Polk & Company. *Nevada State Gazetteer and Business Directory*, 1914-1915. Salt Lake City: R. L. Polk & Company, 1914.

Scrugham, James Graves. *Nevada, a Narrative of* . . . 3 volumes. Chicago: American Historical Society, 1935.

The WPA Guide to 1930's Nevada . . . Reno and Las Vegas: University of Nevada Press, 1991.

Wren, Thomas, ed. *A History of the State of Nevada* . . . New York & Chicago: Lewis Publishing Company, 1904.

Zanjani, Sally. *Goldfield. The Last Gold Rush on the Western Frontier*. Athens, Ohio: Ohio University Press, 1992.

INDEX

Lower case Roman numerals refer to page numbers in the Introduction. Each card that appears in the text has its own number, to which all Arabic numbers refer. Arabic numbers refer to the descriptions that appear for each card, and refer to card numbers, not page numbers

AGE
GILBERT